D1551409

THE PANDA'S BLACK BOX

The Panda's Black Box

OPENING UP THE INTELLIGENT DESIGN CONTROVERSY

EDITED BY NATHANIEL C. COMFORT

Foreword by Daniel J. Kevles

THE JOHNS HOPKINS UNIVERSITY PRESS   Baltimore

© 2007 The Johns Hopkins University Press
All rights reserved. Published 2007
Printed in the United States of America on
acid-free paper
9 8 7 6 5 4 3 2 1

The Johns Hopkins University Press
2715 North Charles Street
Baltimore, Maryland 21218-4363
www.press.jhu.edu

Library of Congress Cataloging-in-Publication Data

The panda's black box: opening up the intelligent
design controversy / Nathaniel C. Comfort, ed.
    p. cm.
Includes bibliographical references (p.   ) and
index.
ISBN-13: 978-0-8018-8599-0 (hardcover : alk. paper)
ISBN-10: 0-8018-8599-x (hardcover : alk. paper)
1. Creationism. 2. Intelligent design (Teleology).
3. Evolution (Biology). 4. Religion and science.
5. Philosophy and science. 6. Science—Philosophy.
I. Comfort, Nathaniel C.
BS652.O64 2007
231.7′652—dc22   2006034764

A catalog record for this book is available from the
British Library.

CONTENTS

CONTRIBUTORS

Nathaniel C. Comfort is an associate professor of the history of medicine at the Johns Hopkins University. He is the author of *The Tangled Field: Barbara McClintock's Search for the Patterns of Genetic Control*. His current research centers on the history of human genetics.

Scott F. Gilbert is a professor of biology at Swarthmore College, teaching embryology, evolutionary developmental biology, and history and critiques of biology. He writes on the history of embryology and genetics, and he authors the textbook *Developmental Biology*. His laboratory research concerns how the turtle got its shell.

Daniel J. Kevles chairs the Program in History of Science and Medicine at Yale University. His works include *In the Name of Eugenics: Genetics and the Uses of Human Heredity*, and he is currently writing a history of intellectual property in living organisms and their parts.

Edward J. Larson is a University Professor in history and holds the Darling Chair in Law at Pepperdine University. He received the 1998 Pulitzer Prize in History for *Summer for the Gods: The Scopes Trial and America's Continuing Debate over Science and Religion* and retains faculty status at the University of Georgia, where he taught for twenty years.

Jane Maienschein is the Regents' Professor and Parents Association Professor at Arizona State University, where she directs the Center for Biology and Society. She is (co)editor of a dozen books and author of three, of which the most recent is *Whose View of Life? Embryos, Cloning, and Stem Cells* (Harvard University Press).

Michael Ruse is a professor of philosophy at Florida State University. He is the author of many books on the history and philosophy of biology, including *The Evolution-Creation Struggle*.

Robert Maxwell Young is a scholar, editor, publisher, and psychotherapist in London. He has taught at the universities of Cambridge, Kent, and Sheffield. He has written on the history and philosophy of ideas of human nature, brain function, Darwinism, Marxism, and psychoanalysis. His writings are online at www.human-nature.com/.

"Teach the controversy," the proponents of Intelligent Design say. By "the controversy," they mean their dispute with Charles Darwin's theory of evolution by natural selection. They claim that such a process, even if it occurred over millions of years, could not possibly have produced something so exquisitely intricate as, say, the human eye. The course of evolution must have been guided by an Intelligent Designer, and the advocates of Intelligent Design have insisted in recent years that it should be given at least a mention as an alternative to Darwin's theory in public school science courses.

The contributors to this volume probe a different controversy: the conflict expressed in the media, school boards, scientific forums, and the courts between the advocates of Intelligent Design and the defenders of Darwin's theory in particular but, more generally, of the content and methods of science. As Nathaniel Comfort notes in his overview of this controversy, the issues in the conflict are broadly intellectual, social, cultural, and religious; they suffuse the dispute over educational policy between those who contend that Intelligent Design belongs in science courses and those who insist that it has no place there—not least because, unlike science, it cannot be refuted. That dispute came to a legal head in a courtroom in Dover, Pennsylvania, where the judge ruled, in December 2005, that Intelligent Design could not be taught as science in the city's schools because it amounted to a religious doctrine.

Like the essays here, the broad conflict has been shadowed by history, including the resistance early in the twentieth century to the teaching of Darwin's theory in the public schools that culminated, in 1925, in the Scopes trial, in Dayton, Tennessee. The resistance movement was mounted by fundamentalist Protestants, partly in response to the modernist disposition to reconcile religion with Darwinism. Yet the antievolution movement was also fired by social tensions. Its enthusiasts, largely white and Anglo-Saxon as well as

Protestant, were centered in the dusty towns of rural America. They resented the city, with its heavy concentrations of Catholics and Jews, of speakeasies and flappers, of science and its intellectually corrosive works. They resented it all the more because urban America was increasingly setting the political and cultural and moral standards of the nation. Its influence was seductively reaching rural youth through mass-circulation magazines, broadcast radio, and movies, and it was thereby undercutting traditional moral values and the authority of religion.

In response to the trend, rural America lashed back, reviving the Ku Klux Klan, demanding that the country remain desolately dry, and following William Jennings Bryan in the revolt against the teaching of evolution that climaxed in the Scopes trial. Demographic trends had encouraged fundamentalists to turn their attention to the schools. Ten times as many students were attending high school in 1920 as in 1890, which meant that ten times as many were vulnerable to exposure to Darwinian doctrines and their corrosion of religious authority. What angered Bryan was the extension of Darwinian evolutionary theory to human beings. To his mind, Darwinism made man too much the product of essentially a material Godless process that invited his degradation through eugenics, too much a competitor in a struggle for survival that justified rapacious business relations and war between nations.

Many observers then and since thought that, even though Scopes lost his case, Bryan, ridiculed on the witness stand by Scopes's counsel Clarence Darrow, lost his cause. But Bryanite religiosity was not shattered by the trial and the country's classrooms were not safeguarded for the teaching of the Darwinian theory of evolution. Antievolutionism, though remaining strong mainly in the South, worked a chilling, nationwide effect on high school biology texts, producing a bowdlerization of the curriculum that continued into the 1950s.

A similar impulse—anti-Darwinism—produced both the Scopes trial and the Dover case. But the battle in the Dover courtroom was fought in a sharply different cultural and religious environment.

Christianity now shares cultural authority in the United States with multiple other religions, which makes it politically difficult to favor one creation story over another in the public schools. And even if Intelligent Design is less a mask for Christian ideas than for religious views of any sort, conservative Christians have been in the vanguard of Intelligent Design and have made it a high-stakes national issue, injecting conflict into the deliberations of school boards as far north as Pennsylvania and once again subjecting curricular policy to lawsuits.

As the Dover court's rejection of Intelligent Design indicates, a robust body of constitutional interpretation has accumulated to keep religious indoctrination out of the schools, especially in science classes, which since the 1960s has eased the task of putting Darwinism into them. The shift in the legal environment led conservative Christians in the 1970s to try to force the teaching of what they called "scientific creationism"—Biblical creation dressed up as science. Rebuffed in the courts, they sought, in ways that Edward Larson delineates in his review of the controversy since Scopes, to acquaint school children with the doctrine of Intelligent Design.

The constitutional environment has done a good deal to reverse the strategy of the antievolutionists. In the era of Scopes, they maneuvered to keep Darwinism out of public education, and they succeeded at the trial in prohibiting discussion of its contents. In the current era, compelled to acknowledge that the teaching of Darwinian evolution in the schools is constitutionally protected, they have resorted to contesting the scientific merits of Darwinism and to offering Intelligent Design as a "scientifically" preferable account of change in organic life. To this end, they have done what the antievolutionists of the Scopes era and the Scopes trial declined to do—employ scientific arguments and expertise on behalf of their cause. Intelligent Design has its own research institution—the Discovery Institute, in the state of Washington—and both a popular and a peer-reviewed technical literature that emphasizes conceptual and evidentiary problems in Darwinian evolution. Its experts include a number of Ph.D.'s in science.

In its employment of technical expertise, Intelligent Design exemplifies a trend that began with economic conservatives in the 1960s in response to the expansion of federal regulation of the environment, health, and safety, all areas entangled with expert knowledge and liberal reformism.[1] In response, conservatives took a leaf from the liberals' book and started organizing their own think tanks, many of them in Washington, D.C., such as the handsomely funded Heritage Foundation and American Enterprise Institute. They went on to establish various science-specific think tanks that fuel conservative ideology with technical information on issues such as global warming. The Discovery Institute is only one of several such enterprises that serve as scientific think tanks for the religious right, addressing issues such as abortion, AIDS, and condom safety.

The theory that human activity is causing global warming may command a consensus of the overwhelming majority of the world's climate scientists, but conservatives combat the claim, with its implications of the imperative need for greater restrictions on the burning of fossil fuels, by stressing the views of a tiny dissenting minority. The religious right also emphasizes claims that fall well outside mainstream science. It insists, for example, that condoms are ineffective in preventing HIV and other sexually transmitted diseases and that abortion elevates the risk of breast cancer or mental illness in women. The expert proponents of Intelligent Design constitute a similarly marginal minority in the world of biology; indeed, most are not even biologists. They exaggerate the scientific significance of their ideas, contending that the idea of design in nature is as revolutionary as the discoveries of, say, Isaac Newton or Albert Einstein. But as Michael Ruse makes clear in his chapter, the ideas expressed by Intelligent Design go back at least to the Greeks, were commonplace through much of the nineteenth century, and compelled the attention of Darwin himself, who conceded that they might have some merit for the ancient initiation of life but declined to believe that design governed the ongoing processes of evolution.

During the Scopes era, leading American scientists, feeling themselves somewhat on the defensive against the onslaught of fundamentalist Protestantism, took pains to emphasize that they saw no conflict between science and religion. For example, in 1923 Robert A. Millikan, the nation's second Nobel laureate in physics and the head of the new California Institute of Technology, drew up a statement that testified not only to the harmony of science and religion but to the value of both. It was released to the newspapers over the signatures of forty-five prominent Americans, including Herbert Hoover and William Allen White, sixteen Protestant theologians, and some of the most distinguished members of the National Academy of Sciences. The dozen leading scientists of the nation had attested to their support of a higher being, Millikan asserted, and he had the documents to prove it.[2]

The nation's current scientific leadership tends to walk a finer line, treating religious authority with deference in its own bailiwick but holding that science and faith operate in wholly different spheres. Many of its members are not Christians and resent the intrusion of Christian-flavored doctrines into science. Many are irritated and some are angered by the Intelligent Design movement's expert claims that Darwinism is inadequate to explain such intricate organs as the eye, a point that Scott Gilbert here refutes in his spirited defense of evolutionary biology. And like Gilbert they hold as specious the movement's assertion that Intelligent Design measures up to the epistemological standards of science.

Their ire has no doubt been reinforced by the religious right's power to interfere with research and policymaking in the biomedical sciences. In the 1920s, the defensiveness of the Millikans may have been offset by the feeling that the future was with modernism and themselves, the priests of the rapidly developing scientific industrial order. Nowadays, the priests of the biomedical sciences feel besieged by the religious right's influence across a broad front of public science. The most salient issue is human stem cell research, the merits of which Jane Maienschein explores in this volume in the context of the controversy over the teaching of evolution. The religious right's political leverage has prompted President George W. Bush to embrace the view that its notion of the controversy over

Intelligent Design should be taught and to impose severe limitations on federal funding of research with human stem cells; and sensitivity to it led the Food and Drug Administration to refuse to approve a so-called morning after pill despite a 23–4 recommendation in favor of approval from its scientific advisers. (Its decision widely attacked, the FDA recanted in August 2006, announcing that the pill would be available over the counter to women 18 and older.)[3] Expressing the scientific community's discontent, at a press conference in February 2004 the Union of Concerned Scientists announced that more than sixty distinguished scientists and government officials, including twenty Nobel laureates, had signed a statement denouncing the Bush administration's misrepresentation and suppression of scientific information and tampering with the scientific advisory process.[4]

Contemporary cosmology, like Darwinian evolution, is beset by evidentiary imperfections, and one can wonder, as Scott Gilbert does, why the Intelligent Designers have not given it equal attention in their schools campaign. One likely reason is that Big Bang theory taught in the schools does not threaten moral, parental, and religious authority in the ways that Darwinism does. On the contrary, the theory that the universe originated in a Big Bang can be taken to support theological accounts of creation, including the Christian version. In 1951, Pope Pius XII celebrated Big Bang theory in an address to the Pontifical Academy of Sciences, declaring contemporary cosmology to mean that "true science to an ever-increasing degree discovers God as though God were waiting behind each closed door opened by science." Indeed, during the 1980s and early 1990s, an avalanche of books and articles appeared drawing religious implications from Big Bang theory. Some of them defended traditional—particularly Christian—religion; others sought satisfaction in a kind of religious cosmological theism.[5]

The maintenance of parental and religious authority has since the 1970s greatly concerned social and religious conservatives. Like their predecessors in the 1920s, they have felt sociocultural anxieties arising from open sexuality and the threat of sexually transmitted diseases and from the legal availability of abortion, contraceptive pills, libertine films and television shows, and pornography on the Internet. They are troubled by modern biology's seeming drive to reduce living beings to molecules and their morally purposeless interactions, a drive that, as Robert Young iconoclastically argues here, by no means succeeded in Darwin's day and has not succeeded entirely in ours either. Many also find unsettling the challenges to human values and dignity in the manipulative abilities of modern biology, in its emerging powers of human genetic engineering and its present powers to intervene in human life from the womb to the deathbed.

In its popularity, the Intelligent Design movement thus reveals deep-seated tensions in the politics and power of the biomedical sciences in the context of the profound sociocultural changes that have marked American society since the 1970s. While the essays in this volume do not give quarter to the doctrine of Intelligent Design, they seek to thread a path of understanding through its tangled engagements and to replace with illuminating reason the dogmatism found on both sides of the controversy. They have succeeded handsomely in both these purposes, and more.

THE PANDA'S BLACK BOX

Introduction

The Panda's Black Box

NATHANIEL C. COMFORT

When the topic of the Intelligent Design controversy comes up, my biologist-friends often shrug and laugh, "What controversy?" This remark illustrates two key themes. First, among biologists, there is no controversy over Intelligent Design. There are real controversies within evolutionary biology, such as over the role and importance of neutral evolution versus natural selection and over the relative importance of molecular and fossil data. But ID is not one of them. Biologists—whether atheist, animist, Muslim, Hindu, Christian, or Jewish—simply do not take Intelligent Design seriously as an evolutionary mechanism. Second, the remark reflects a contempt for the larger controversy of which Intelligent Design is only a part. Science has been the dominant cultural enterprise of the twentieth century, and biology is now the queen of the sciences. The basic claims of biology—the evolution of life, the role of genes in heredity, the material basis of mind—are as well supported as the claim that the earth revolves around the sun. As a consequence, it has become easy to believe that biology can explain anything about any living thing. In recent years, we have seen biological explanations seep into such unlikely venues as international relations, literature, and even religion itself. The biological worldview is so well supported by evidence, so coherent theoretically, so compelling to anyone not dogmatically mystical, that many of those insulated by ivy-covered laboratory walls find it inconceivable that anyone would challenge it. Yet challenge it they do, and when the scientific community dismisses the challengers as either ignorant or stupid, the public—many of whom accept science's authority in matters of nature but not of morals—tends to see the disingenuous design proponents as paragons of intellectual honesty and integrity. Religion and science may be reconcilable philosophically, but they are locked in a war for cultural authority.

To be sure, science has its activists—bright, worldly, politically sophisticated observers and spokesmen—and they are deeply, perhaps rightly, concerned about the status of science. But they are a minority. Most scientists prefer to practice their politics in the circumscribed worlds of the department, university, and funding agencies and committees, rather than on the public stage.

"Teach the controversy," say the design proponents. They claim only to want fair, open-minded discussion of the alternatives to Darwinian evolution in public biology classrooms. Their principal tool for teaching the controversy is the "supplemental" textbook *Of Pandas and People*. The panda became the emblem of Intelligent Design in 2005, after Mike Argento, a columnist for the York, Pennsylvania, *Daily Record*, dubbed the Intelligent Design trial in Dover the "Panda trial." Yet teaching the controversy in biology class puts the panda in a black box. It deliberately misconstrues "the controversy" as being about the biological evidence and so masks the larger cultural and political debate with scientific language.

By all means, let us teach the controversy—but not in biology class. We need the tools of the humanities to peel away the rhetoric and the politics, to see what the controversy is really about. We must open the panda's black box. Let us begin by recognizing the controversy as a debate between *anti*-Darwinists and *anti*-creationists, rather than creationists and evolutionists. Not all creationists are anti-Darwinists and not all evolutionists are anticreationists. The debate is between a small, highly vocal subset of the populations each side claims to represent. Recalling this is the first step in resolving the apparent paradox of how such an antiscientific movement could garner so much attention at a historical moment when the life sciences have achieved unprecedented status and power.

_____

One point on which anti-Darwinists and anticreationists agree is that this is a pitched battle between dogmatic religious fanatics on the one hand, and rigorous, fair-minded scientists on the other. However, which side is which depends on who you read. In *Darwin's Dangerous Idea*, the philosopher and ardent anticreationist Daniel Dennett wrote that there were "no forces on this planet more dangerous to us all than the fanaticisms of fundamentalism" and followed with a discussion of the creation scientists' campaign to have creation science taught alongside evolution in schools. But Dennett himself has been called a fundamentalist—and by no less than the distinguished evolutionist Stephen Jay Gould. Reviewing *The Devil's Chaplain* by the English evolutionist and anticreationist Richard Dawkins, Michael Ruse called Dawkins "the atheist's answer to Billy Graham." Anti-Darwinists delight in such table-turning and rarely miss a chance to cast their opponents as fundamentalist fanatics. George Gilder, cofounder of the Discovery Institute, the epicenter of the ID movement, wrote, "To parallel 'Inherit the Wind,' it's the materialists who are the religious fanatics this time. They want to stomp on their critics." In *Darwin on Trial* (1991), a founding text of ID, Phillip Johnson distanced himself from fundamentalism, writing, "I am not a defender of creation-science . . . I assume that the creation-scientists are biased by their pre-commitment to Biblical fundamentalism, and I will have very little to say about their position." His goal in the book was to investigate whether Darwinism, too, was "another kind of fundamentalism." In this debate, then, fundamentalism stands for dogmatism, closed-mindedness, and superstition.[1]

Science, in contrast, stands for reason, fairness, objectivity, and adherence to demonstrable fact. The anti-Darwinists drape themselves in the mantle of science, damning their opponents as mystics and mountebanks. In his 1996 *Darwin's Black Box*, Michael Behe, a biochemist and a leading design proponent, pounced on biochemical studies that are qualitative rather than quantitative: "Without numbers, there is no science." Elsewhere, he claimed flatly that "molecular evolution is not based on scientific authority." Johnson, in *Darwin on Trial*, portrayed paleontologists as needing "to find a theory that would allow them to report their projects as successful," a kind of reasoning from the conclusions that is anathema to good science. Johnson goes on to call neo-Darwinism "pseudo-science," a derogatory term scientists have long used to denote ideological, superstitious, or fraudulent science: phrenology, astrology, the worst forms of eugenics, and the like. Richard John Neuhaus, a Discovery Institute fellow, contrasted the biologists' "quasi-religious establishment of a narrow evolutionary theory" with the design proponents' "rational and scientific course" of presenting all sides of the debate. In a similar vein, David Limbaugh, another Discovery Institute fellow, railed at "academics" who hold "strong, secular predispositions that must be guarded with a blind religious fervor. Indeed, it appears many Darwinists are guilty of precisely that of which they accuse ID proponents: having a set of preconceived assumptions that taint their scientific objectivity." In *The Design Revolution*, William Dembski, another leading design theorist, calls Darwinism a "magic gig," and says it is nothing but tricks. He refers to "the smokescreens and the hand-waving, the just-so stories and the stonewalling, the bluster and the bluffing" that he says constitute evolutionary theory.[2]

Design proponents also exploit the rhetorical power of scientific presentations. Whereas the anticreationist Richard Dawkins illustrates his books like a naturalist, with evolutionary trees and images of plants and animals, the design proponents favor illustrations characteristic of "harder" sciences and engineering. Michael Behe employs data tables and schematic drawings of molecules and molecular pathways. William Dembski publishes flow charts that look like circuit diagrams. Stuart Pullen chocked his recent book *Intelligent Design or Evolution?* full of stark, angular diagrams that make it resemble a physics text. Design proponents exploit graphics to create a sense of rigorous hard science.

Credibility is vital in any scientific debate. Although Michael Behe is the only practicing bench scientist among the movement's leaders, the ID movement boasts the doctorates of William Dembski (mathematics), Jonathan Wells (biology), and Stephen Meyer (history and philosophy of science), as well as "graduate degrees" (presumably mostly masters') of others. The Discovery Institute gathered the signatures of 514 Ph.D. scientists on a petition expressing skepticism "of claims for the ability of random mutation and natural selection to account for the complexity of life." But the core of scientific credibility is the peer-review process. Scientists have a rather narrow definition of peer review: a peer-reviewed article is one that has been reviewed *favorably* by two or more qualified researchers; the reviewers' criticisms have been addressed; and the article has been accepted by an editorial board and then published by the same journal that reviewed it. The design proponents count as peer-reviewed anything that was read by another design proponent, whether or not the review process was open to critics of ID, whether or not the peers rejected the article, or where it was published. On its website, the Discovery Institute lists dozens of publications on or supporting Intelligent Design under headings such as "peer-reviewed articles," "articles in peer-reviewed journals" (not the same thing), and "articles supportive of Intelligent Design published in peer-edited scientific anthologies and conference proceedings." The Discovery Institute site also lists book reviews, retracted articles, and trade books. Many publications are multiply listed in order to lengthen the list. Such tactics reflect a rather desperate desire for the appearance of scientific credibility.

Science, of course, is the anticreationists' home turf, so it is curious that they resort to sarcasm, derogation, and name-calling in defending it. Dawkins again provides some of the best quotations, but he is hardly alone. In *The Ancestor's Tale*, he mentioned how "creationists go on (as they tediously do) about 'gaps' in the fossil record" (13). In Dawkins's hands, even that dry bit of scholarly apparatus, the index, becomes a weapon. The reader can locate a reference to the preceding quotation under "Creationists → Going on about 'gaps'"; the entry for "'Intelligent design theorist'" (in quotes) reads simply, "See Creationist." Elsewhere, Dawkins refers to creationists' "carefully impoverished imaginations" and calls Behe's "Argument from Irreducible Complexity"—a theoretical mainstay of ID—the "Argument from Personal Incredulity." With Menckenesque alliteration, Daniel Dennett called creation science a "pathetic hodge-podge of pious pseudo-science." The National Center for Science Education, the nation's leading anticreationist organization, satirizes the Discovery Institute's "Dissent from Darwin" petition with its 514 signatories with "Project Steve," in homage to Stephen Jay Gould. As of March 7, 2006, they had compiled a list of 726 Ph.D. scientists who have gone on record supporting evolution—all named Steve. Anticreationists delight in putting forward tongue-in-cheek "theories" of creation, from the Invisible Pink Unicorn to the Flying Spaghetti Monster, which they insist have as much scientific validity as Intelligent Design.[3]

(Lest the design proponents be pilloried as humorless, William Dembski has created "Panda-monium," a video game in which— once again—he turns the tables, portraying anticreationists as pandas, which drop from the sky, spewing slogans such as "Intelligent design is just creationism in a cheap tuxedo!" while the player shoots at them from a tank.)[4]

The anticreationists' rhetoric carries more than a note of condescension. Dawkins wrote in a letter to the *New York Review of Books*, "No qualified scientist doubts that evolution is a fact . . . No reputable biologist doubts this." Dawkins seems to suggest that to be a reputable biologist is to accept evolution; the point he is ostensibly defending is almost axiomatic. In what must be the most highly quoted passage in the ID literature, from a 1989 book review in the *New York Times*, Dawkins wrote, "It is absolutely safe to say that if you meet somebody who claims not to believe in evolution, that person is ignorant, stupid or insane (or wicked, but I'd rather not consider that)." Referring to design proponents, in a 2005 essay called "Show

Me the Science," Dennett wrote, "It takes scientific discipline to protect ourselves from our own credulity, but we've also found ingenious ways to fool ourselves and others."[5]

The anticreationists' contempt leaves the anti-Darwinists an easy strategy: they turn to the audience with saucer eyes and outstretched arms and simply ask for a hearing and honest debate. "Don't academics purport to champion free and open inquiry?" wrote David Limbaugh. "What, then, are they so afraid of regarding the innocuous introduction into the classroom of legitimate questions concerning Darwinism?" There is nothing innocuous or legitimate about it. Yet the nonscientific public, unable to distinguish inquiry from sophistry through the scientific smokescreen, thinks this a legitimate request. Anticreationist scientists often refuse invitations to debate the anti-Darwinists, insisting that there is no serious scientific debate to be had. They are in a no-win bind. If they debate, they give publicity and legitimacy to an opponent they do not respect; yet if they refuse, they seem arrogant.

———————

Release from the bind would come through recognition that, although the controversy is couched in the language and standards of science, it is not about the findings of science. Rather, it is about the place of science in society. Among the many strains of anti-Darwinism—Biblical literalism, creation science, and the like—the design proponents stand out for the extent to which they use science to advance a deeply antiscientific view.

The venue for their campaign, of course, is public biology education. For most of a century, anti-Darwinists have fought the teaching of evolution in public schools. Although they have won a few battles, the front has moved steadily backward. The state of Tennessee banned the teaching of evolution in 1925, followed by Mississippi and Arkansas. In the 1968 case *Epperson v. Arkansas*, the U.S. Supreme Court struck down the Arkansas law, on grounds that it violated the Establishment Clause of the First Amendment, which prohibits state establishment of religion. Prevented from banning the teaching of evolution outright, the anti-Darwinists sought to dilute it with creationism. Tennessee again led the way, with a state law requiring public schools to give equal emphasis to the Genesis account in the Bible and demanding that evolution be taught as theory, not as fact. This, too, was declared unconstitutional, in 1975. The 1961 book *Genesis Flood*, by John C. Whitcomb and Henry Morris, provided a basis for so-called creation science, which sought to defend the Genesis story on purely scientific (mainly geological) grounds. In the early 1980s, Arkansas and Louisiana passed "balanced treatment" laws mandating the teaching of creation science in equal measure with evolution. The Arkansas law expressly excluded the teaching of religion and limited the teaching of both theories to scientific data. Nevertheless, in 1982 a federal judge saw it as an attempt to smuggle theology into the classroom and ruled it unconstitutional, again as a violation of the Establishment Clause. The Supreme Court's 1987 *Edwards v. Aguillard* decision struck down Louisiana's balanced treatment law on the same grounds. Yet creation science was sufficiently successful that anticreationist lobbying groups sprang up across the country. In 1983, these groups merged into the National Center for Science Education, whose primary purpose was and is to resist opposition to the teaching of evolution.

Immediately on the heels of the *Edwards* decision came the first stirrings of Intelligent Design. The change of tack came so suddenly that a creation science textbook, *Biology and Origins* (originally, *Creation Biology*), in preparation when the decision was handed down, required a quick editorial makeover. It was renamed *Of Pandas and People*, and references to "creationism" and "creationists" were removed and "intelligent design" and "design proponents" substituted. The editing was so hasty that, in one case, only the middle of "creationists" was removed, leading to the revealing typo "cdesign proponentsists" in a *Pandas* draft. Ironically, molecular evolutionists exploit just this sort of editorial trace in our genomes to reconstruct life's history.[6]

Prohibited from requiring "balanced treatment," anti-Darwinists today claim to seek only the freedom to discuss alternatives to evolution: the "teach the controversy" strategy. Science standards in several states embrace this approach. In order to do so, most, like Kansas, find it necessary to redefine science as a kind of medieval activity, with natural and supernatural explanations carrying equal weight. And yet the recent high-profile decisions in Dover, Pennsylvania, and in Columbus, Ohio, have dealt severe blows to anti-Darwinists. This give and take should not mask the larger trend: rhetorically, the anti-Darwinists have backtracked steadily, compensating for a weaker position with greater force and cleverness in their arguments.

Thus, only vestiges of creationism remain in the public case for anti-Darwinism. On the current trajectory, one can imagine an anti-Darwinism so feeble that the Supreme Court cannot ban it. This does not mean anti-Darwinism has become powerless: the so-called Wedge Strategy, the manifesto written in 1998 and posted on the Internet in 1999, produced by the Discovery Institute's Center for the Renewal of Science and Culture, seeks to make anti-Darwinism superficially indistinguishable from science, and thereby to gain access for more strongly theistic doctrines in the public schools. ID's intellectual anemia turns out to be a powerful rhetorical strategy: unless you know your biology, it seems quite reasonable. Nearly all anti-Darwinists today admit extensive microevolution, which explains things like the evolution of bacteria that are resistant to antibiotics, as distinct from macroevolution, which explains the creation of new species and higher taxonomic groups. Michael Behe concedes that natural selection has been the driving force for much of evolution and has even admitted, to the Christian Darwinist Kenneth Miller, that he accepts the common ancestry of man and apes. The ID textbook, *Of Pandas and People*, concedes Darwin's first argument, that speciation is analogous to what breeders do, but denies that speciation is evolution (19–20). Anti-Darwinists have never conceded so much to their opponents. The Discovery Institute's George Gilder inadvertently revealed how weak Intelligent Design's anti-

Darwinism was when he told the *Boston Globe*, "What's being pushed is to have Darwinism critiqued, to teach there's a controversy. Intelligent design itself does not have any content."[7]

Biologists tend to agree with Gilder that ID has no content. We should not, however, make the mistake of believing it wholly vacuous. Whether or not one believes Intelligent Design misguided as a worldview, it is folly to ignore it as social critique. Some of this critique stems from an unreflective traditionalism: modern biology is profoundly changing our relationship to ourselves and to each other, and that makes many people uneasy. But another part of the critique stems from a well-founded nervousness about biology as the basis of morality and ethics. As Michael Specter pointed out in the *New Yorker* magazine, the extraordinary power (and even more sensational promise and hype) of biology in the twenty-first century can be frightening.[8]

Thus, there are both theological and secular reasons to critique the cultural role of biology. By blurring the distinction between them, the design proponents create a big tent. However, if we separate them, we can see some of the sources of ID's appeal, which can otherwise seem paradoxical in this age of science. One can sympathize with aspects of the cultural critique of science without advocating Intelligent Design—or demonizing science.

Design proponents couch their critique in terms of an assault on "materialism," a philosophical term referring to the belief that all phenomena can be explained in physical terms. Materialism is an ancient philosophy that can be dated to the ancient Greeks and that bloomed during the Enlightenment. It has acquired many meanings over the centuries, and some of them are perfectly compatible with theism. Anti-Darwinists, however, have lumped the various materialisms to give them a political cast. The "wedge" document held that a materialistic conception of reality "infected virtually every area of our culture, with devastating consequences," particularly by denying the existence of objective moral standards. The document's strategy is frankly revolutionary: its authors sought "nothing less than the overthrow of materialism and its cultural legacies."[9]

Some of the wedge document's rhetorical force stems from getting its history wrong. It falsely credits the origin of materialism to Darwin, Freud, and Karl Marx. Marx, of course, originated *dialectical* materialism, which stresses the struggle between opposites as the mechanism for progress. Crediting Marx and Darwin with inventing materialism allows anti-Darwinists to link evolution to communism. The anti-Darwinists' focus on "materialism," then, is politically expedient, intended to win over moderate conservatives to their cause of linking science to moral relativism. (It has not, however, won over certain hard-headed conservatives, such as Charles Krauthammer and George Will, not to mention Judge John E. Jones III, who presided in Dover. In this atomized age, not all conservatives believe that the way to institutionalize morality is by attacking the foundations of science.)[10]

Darwin, Marx, and Freud are profoundly secular figures, whose collective legacy is the replacement of religious authority with scientific authority. Darwin made a science of creation; Freud made a science of the mind; and Marx made a science of society. Science has a mixed record as a guide for social change. In some spheres, the advantages are undeniable. Only an extremist sectarian would choose an amulet over an antibiotic to treat an infection. God denied man wings, but NASA put him on the moon. And yet, with science's authority has come a kind of hubris, a belief that true knowledge can come only from natural science and therefore that science can solve all social problems. This belief is called *scientism*. Therein lies science's darker legacy—and the source of the secular critique of science.

Eugenics and social Darwinism—two of the design proponents' favorite examples of the destructiveness of so-called materialism— were deeply scientistic. They emerged in the late nineteenth and early twentieth centuries, a time of tremendous scientific discovery and, increasingly by the 1890s, a sense that science could be used to solve social problems. Social Darwinists, such as William Graham Sumner, argued for a social theory built on principles of competition and survival of the fittest derived from Darwin and, more directly, his contemporary Herbert Spencer. Sumner perverted Darwin's notion of fitness, casting it not as reproductive success but as economic success. With Sumner, the wealthy—the least reproductively successful in Darwinian terms—became the most fit while the prolific poor were recast as the unfit. Thus, Sumner could argue on scientific grounds for the abolition of social welfare, progressive income tax, protective tariffs, and other forms of government intervention intended to level the playing field. In contrast, eugenics, in its heyday, was the doctrine that social problems from disease to poverty to crime were rooted ultimately in bad heredity; improving the germ plasm (gene pool) was the route to a better society.

In a way, eugenics and social Darwinism are more closely related now than they were a century ago. Since the 1930s, genetics and evolution have been united as complementary parts of science's explanation of biological change. Evolution is genetic and genetics is evolutionary. Any critique of evolutionary biology today necessarily implicates genetics as well. Indeed, modern forms of biological scientism draw considerable potency from the genetic notion of innateness. Thus, there is a thread of historical continuity within the social critique of biology.

Although social Darwinism is long discredited, in its place we have what we may call "cultural Darwinism." Social Darwinism applied evolutionary thinking to social and economic problems. Cultural Darwinism applies it to almost any aspect of modern culture. It is a species of scientism that emphasizes evolutionary thought—and exploits the genetic notion of innateness. In *The Blind Watchmaker*, Richard Dawkins extended to culture the notion of genes as units of heredity. He coined the term "memes," to denote an idea that spreads through a cultural equivalent of natural selection. Darwinism applies to culture, Dawkins said. Since then, many authors have applied Darwinism to an extraordinary range of fields well outside the realm of biology. The scientific content of nonbiological Darwinism is often elementary and old-fashioned. The stodginess of the science indicates the trendiness of the idea, because few of these authors have done more than skim off a Darwinian concept or two. Armchair Darwinizing misrepresents and distorts biological reasoning, with consequences that are sometimes comical, sometimes chilling.

Much cultural Darwinism is rooted in Darwin's notion of a struggle for existence, borrowed from the Reverend Thomas Malthus, the nineteenth-century political economist. This sense of Darwinism is the direct offspring of Spencer's and Sumner's social Darwinism. The more entrepreneurial, competitive, and cut-throat a business is, the more Darwinian it is said to be. Evan Schwartz's recent book, *Digital Darwinism*, paraphrases Darwin's argument in business lingo: Darwin, he writes, described a world in which species "must continue to grow in a profitable direction and develop new skills and traits or perish."[11] This lexicon applies to the digital business landscape of the World Wide Web, he says. The language of Darwinism adds no content to the argument—"ruthless," "competitive," or "Malthusian" would do just as well. Rather, to call this Darwinism gives it a kind of cachet. It expresses Darwinism's cultural power, without hefting its intellectual weight.

As nineteenth-century social Darwinists knew, evolutionary explanations are convenient for justifying the status quo. In *Darwinian Politics: The Evolutionary Origins of Freedom*, the Emory University economist Paul Rubin argues that the fact that men—he calls us "males"—can father more children than women can bear makes them more willing to take risks and therefore more political than women—er, "females."[12] He reaches the "surprising conclusion" that people fortunate to live in Western society and the United States are happier than everyone else, because our higher incomes and better technology allow us to satisfy our evolutionarily encoded drives and tastes.

More substantive applications of Darwinism are varieties of adaptationism, the notion that almost any trait can be explained as an evolutionary adaptation to a past environment. Adaptationism is actually pre-Darwinian, with roots in the eighteenth-century philosophical position known as natural theology. But the modern language of evolutionary genetics gives adaptationism great new prestige. Belittled by Stephen Jay Gould as "just-so stories," adaptationist arguments propose plausible but sometimes specious or untestable evolutionary explanations of particular traits. The danger for Gould was that they masked alternative evolutionary mechanisms and therefore led to bad science. But when applied to human affairs, Darwinian just-so stories can be vacuous, culturally impoverishing, or downright dangerous.

A minor wave currently washing through our English departments, "literary Darwinism" seeks to use evolutionary psychology to explain authors' motives in writing novels, or even to interpret those novels. Thus, Brian Boyd gives us *Hamlet* explained in terms of "the necessity and intensity of retributive feelings in social animals," and Joseph Carroll interprets *Pride and Prejudice* as a story about men's desire to acquire resources and use them to acquire mates, and women's seeking of mates who are in possession of resources. Recently, Bradley Thayer has applied adaptationist logic to industrial relations and warfare. Evolutionary theory, he writes, "provides an ultimate causal explanation for warfare." He distills the insights this perspective provides thus: "The essence of my argument is that people wage war to gain and defend resources. Thus evolutionary theory provides a sufficient cause of warfare."[13]

In other cases, armchair evolutionists collapse complex social processes into brute drives. In *Darwinian Psychiatry*, Michael McGuire and Alfonso Troisi explain suicide "as a form of kin-related altruism," or, alternatively, as a response to a failure to achieve reproductive goals. Men beat their wives, the authors suggest, to make intimacy predictable, paternity certain, child care assured, and to improve their self-esteem and social status.[14]

The Harvard entomologist Edward O. Wilson spearheads what may be the most sweeping effort yet to include all of culture under the evolutionary tent. In his 1998 book, *Consilience*, he outlined a congenial-sounding plan to unite the sciences and the humanities under the book's eponymous concept. In fact, however, the reader soon discovers that Wilson's vision is that biology *explains* the humanities. Art, music, literature, and philosophy result from primal evolutionary drives. Rather than uniting the sciences and humanities, consilience seeks to subsume the humanities under the umbrella of science. Examining Wilson's rhetoric in *Consilience*, the rhetorician Leah Ceccarelli found that he relied on "frontier-era images of exploration and conquest" and even colonialism, with natural scientists portrayed as the explorers and missionaries and social scientists as the primitive savages, in need of civilization. Wilson's consilience is about the conquest of culture by science.[15]

The coup de grace is to explain religion itself in Darwinian terms. In *Consilience*, Wilson wrote, "Every major religion today is a winner in the Darwinian struggle waged among cultures, and none ever flourished by tolerating its rivals." In 2000, the professional skeptic Michael Shermer published *How We Believe*, a sociological meditation, complete with survey data, on the patterns of religious belief. Anthropologists have turned the tables on the Creator and the created, as shown by titles such as Pascal Boyer's *And Man Creates God: Religion Explained* (2001) and Scott Atran's *In Gods We Trust* (2002). Also in 2002, David Sloan Wilson published *Darwin's Cathedral*, which treats religions as organisms and their cultural evolution as a kind of group selection. Daniel Dennett's latest book, *Breaking the Spell: Religion as a Natural Phenomenon*, attempts an evolutionay explanation of religion, and the title of Dawkins's latest effort, *The God Delusion*, speaks for itself. Such authors have genetics on their side. A recent article by L. B. Koenig and others at the University of Minnesota claimed to have identified a gene that confers spiritual inclination—it was immediately dubbed the "religion gene."[16]

This is not to say that these behaviors have no biological basis; rather, the biology is trivial and unhelpful. In their scientistic drive for "ultimate causal explanations" of complex social phenomena such as suicide, warfare, art, or spirituality, these Darwinian excursions conclude their inquiry at precisely the point at which their subject begins to require explanation: the moment when it transcends biology and takes on the complexity that makes violence tragic and literature moving.

_____

In short, Darwinism itself has become a meme. The power of Darwin's theory is so great that it tends to outcompete other ideas, to adapt to new and extreme environments. Paired with a genetic understanding of heredity, it appears to explain almost anything. It is not irrational to be concerned about the encroachment of scientific authority into all aspects of life—and such concern need not make one antiscience or anti-intellectual.

Intelligent Design seduces because it seems to walk this middle ground. By cloaking a critique of the cultural authority of biology in scientific robes, it offers an option to the educated laity who embrace science as both authoritative and progressive and yet reject full-throated scientism. It appeals to those who harbor a malaise, however inarticulate, over the cultural dominance of science and yet who still vaccinate their kids. For some, ID's critique of scientific cultural authority implies a restoration of religious cultural authority—and so it wins over far-right religious conservatives. But the carefully vague language in *Pandas* and other ID texts leaves room for more secular skeptics of science as well.

The irony is that Intelligent Design in fact exemplifies scientism. Its appeal is independent of the validity (or lack thereof) of its fact claims. Its authority rests entirely on its ability to mount scientific-sounding cases and make them sound persuasive—on scientific rhetoric rather than scientific evidence. By adopting scientific trappings, as well as by playing laboratory shell games in which they claim to disprove unequivocal results, the design theorists become co-opted by the very forces they oppose. In short, even while ID attacks science, it accepts science's authority. Of all the forms of anti-Darwinism since Darwin, ID is the most scientistic.

It is no mystery, then, why Intelligent Design flourishes in an age of dramatic biomedical advance. Viewing through the lens of cultural Darwinism, we would *expect* to see a resurgence of anti-

Darwinism in the genome age, and we would expect it to be the most secular, scientific version of anti-Darwinism yet. We would not necessarily expect the scientists to differentiate between legitimate and illegitimate challenges to their authority. It is in their interest, too, to keep the debate focused on the narrow questions of scientific data. Biologists, who by and large are well funded and secure, are particularly well insulated from dissident views, however common those views may be in the outside world. The wind may howl outside, but it is snug indoors. Feeling fortified against the storm, in a house one helped build, one might well look around at the solid walls, the tight sashes, the fast latches, and say, half humorously, half proudly, "What storm?"

The Argument from Design

MICHAEL RUSE

In 1802, opening his book *Natural Theology* with one of the most famous passages in the history of philosophy, Archdeacon William Paley wrote:

> In crossing a heath suppose I pitched my foot against a stone, and were asked how the stone came to be there, I might possibly answer, that for any thing I knew to the contrary it had lain there for ever; nor would it, perhaps, be very easy to show the absurdity of this answer. But supposing I had found a watch upon the ground, and it should be inquired how the watch happened to be in that place, I should hardly think of the answer which I had before given, that for any thing I knew the watch might have always been there. Yet why should not this answer serve for the watch as well as for the stone; why is it not as admissible in the second case as in the first? For this reason, and for no other, namely, that when we come to inspect the watch, we perceive—what we could not discover in the stone—that its several parts are framed and put together for a purpose, e.g. that they are so formed and adjusted as to produce motion, and that motion so regulated as to point out the hour of the day; that if the different parts had been shaped different from what they are, or placed after any other manner or in any other order than that in which they are placed, either no motion at all would have been carried on in the ma-

chine, or none which would have answered the use that is now served by it.[1]

This is the opening move to the well-known Argument from Design (also known as the Teleological Argument) for the existence of a god, or rather of the Christian God. A watch implies a watch-maker. Likewise, the adaptations of the living world imply an adaptation maker, a deity. You cannot argue otherwise without falling into absurdity. "This is atheism; for every indication of contrivance, every manifestation of design which existed in the watch, exists in the works of nature, with the difference on the side of nature of being greater and more, and that in a degree which exceeds all computation."[2]

So influential and widely read was Paley that his book was part of the final examinations at the University of Cambridge until after the First World War. Yet even as he wrote, the argument was under heavy attack and this continued through the nineteenth century. The great theologian John Henry Newman, who began his life as an evangelical Anglican, moving through the High Church and then on to Rome, and eventually a cardinal's hat, wrote in 1870 (twenty-five years after he converted), in correspondence about his seminal philosophical work *A Grammar of Assent*: "I have not insisted on the argument from *design*, because I am writing for the 19th century, by which, as represented by its philosophers, design is not admitted as proved. And to tell the truth, though I should not wish to preach on the subject, for 40 years I have been unable to see the logical force of the argument myself. I believe in design because I believe in God; not in a God because I see design." He continued: "Design teaches me power, skill and goodness—not sanctity, not mercy, not a future judgment, which three are of the essence of religion."[3]

Not all agree with Newman. Indeed today the Argument from Design is as popular as ever, especially in American evangelical circles. So, because the best way to understand the present is always by looking to the past, let us go back to the earliest days of the argument, and follow its fortunes through to the twenty-first century. I am not so much concerned here to criticize today's supporters of the argument, as to put their enthusiasm into context and warn that one should realize that however new things may now seem, they have a long and relevant history.

THE GREEKS

Plato gives the first explicit discussion of the argument in his great dialogue (the *Phaedo*) centered on the death of Socrates. Asked why he does not fear death, the old man replies that either it is dreamless sleep or a good god exists and there is something pretty good in the future. Then Socrates goes on to provide arguments for the existence of this god. Plato, through his mouthpiece Socrates, invites us to consider artifacts. We know that they could not have come into being through blind chance. There must have been a designer. The same is true also of organisms. They could not have come into being through blind chance. There must have been a designer, a being that in a later dialogue (the *Timaeus*) Plato called the Demiurge.

This was also the line of Plato's student, the philosopher Aristotle. He argued that we must take seriously the notion of "final cause" (as opposed especially to "efficient cause"), meaning by this that living things seem put together for specific ends, namely, the good of the organisms themselves. Explicitly, Aristotle criticized those physiologists who think that discussion of causation ends with reference to the immediate causes of features. He asked: "What are the forces by which the hand or the body was fashioned into its shape?" An artisan (speaking of a copy or model) would answer that the forces were the tools like an axe or an auger. But this is not enough. Simple reference to the tools and their effects leaves unanswered questions. One must bring in ends. The woodcarver "must state the reasons why he struck his blow in such a way as to effect this, and for the sake of what he did so; namely, that the piece of wood should develop eventually into this or that shape." In like manner against the physiologists, "the true method is to state what the characters are that distinguish the animal—to explain what it is and what are its qualities—and to deal after the same fashion with its several parts; in fact, to proceed in exactly the same way as we should do, were we dealing with the form of a couch" (*Parts of Animals*, 641a 7–17).[4]

It is useful to distinguish two moves being made in the argument. First, there is the drawing attention to something special, something complex, something that needs explaining. From the *Phaedo*: "I had formerly thought that it was clear to everyone that he grew through eating and drinking; that when, through food, new flesh and bones came into being to supplement the old, and thus in the same way each kind of thing was supplemented by new substances proper to it, only then did the mass which was small become large, and in the same way the small man big" (96d). Flesh and bones don't just happen. In the real world, things rust and decay and mess up. Socrates would have been appreciative of Murphy's Law: "If something can go wrong, it will." Blind law leads to randomness. Let us talk of the postulation (or discovery) of this something that needs explaining as the "argument to complexity."

Then there is the explanation of this complexity. But notice that it is not just complexity in the sense of being intricate. It is complexity in the sense of speaking to ends. The *Phaedo* again: "The ordering Mind ordered everything and placed each thing severally as it was best that it should be; so that if anyone wanted to discover the cause of anything, how it came into being or perished or existed, he simply needed to discover what kind of existence was best for it, or what it was best that it should do or have done to it" (97b–c). The way we explain this complexity is by postulating an intelligence. Let us call this the "argument to design." (There is the potential for confusion here. The overall argument is usually called the "Argument from Design," meaning that the world is designed, and hence there is a designer. Really though the crucial moves are to say that the world is design-like, and that the explanation must be a designer. I am not in the business of reforming language. Normally, I will follow convention referring to the overall argument as the "Argument from Design.")

One point of historical importance centers on the complex. Plato clearly thought that complexity in the sense we talk of now is to be found in the inorganic world as well as the organic world. The hand or the eye is complex. So also are the planets in their movements through the heavens. Both kinds of phenomena speak to the deity. Aristotle is not so clear. When he introduces the notion of final cause, it seems to apply indifferently to the inorganic and the organic. But in his explicitly biological discussions, he rather implies that it is only in the organic world that we find final cause. The whole point about biological complexity is that it is end-directed, and most obviously it is end-directed when it is helping its possessor. An eye is of value to an individual because then there is sight. An ear is of value, because then there is hearing. It is not obvious to see how a planet in motion, however intricate, is of value—is speaking to an end. Hence, often (if not always) for Aristotle complexity is exclusively a biological phenomenon. It is organisms that lead us to a god.

THE CHRISTIANS

Obviously for Plato and Aristotle this was not the Christian God. Indeed, Aristotle's chief god is a particularly unsympathetic sort of fellow—an unmoved Mover, who is unaware of our existence and spends all of His time contemplating His own perfection. However the Argument from Design was taken up by the great Christian philosophers, who were greatly influenced by Greek thought. Saint Augustine talked about it in his fifth-century work, *The City of God*: "the world itself, by the perfect order of its changes and motions, and by the great beauty of all things visible, proclaims by a kind of silent testimony of its own both that it has been created, and also that it could not have been made other than by a God ineffable and invisible in greatness, and ineffable and invisible in beauty."[5] Nearly a thousand years later, the argument achieved canonical status from Saint Thomas Aquinas, who highlighted it as one of five proofs of God's existence. He began, "We see that things that lack intelligence, such as natural bodies, act for an end, and this is evident from their acting always, or nearly always, in the same way, so as to obtain the best result. Hence it is plain that not fortuitously, but designedly do they [things of this world] achieve their end." Then from this premise (equivalent of the argument to organization), more claimed than defended, we move to the Creator behind things (argument to design). "Now whatever lacks knowledge cannot move towards an end, unless it is directed by some being endowed with knowledge and intelligence; as the arrow is shot to its mark by the archer. Therefore some intelligent being exists by which all natural things are directed to their end; and this being we call God."[6]

Important though this argument was, one should be careful not to take it out of historical context. Augustine and Aquinas would not have gone so far as Newman—they thought the argument worked, and Augustine particularly (much influenced by Plato) would have argued for the transcendent aspects of the Godhead—but they would have agreed that it is no substitute for faith. It—and indeed the whole "natural theological" project of getting at God through reason—always takes back place to God as understood through the authority of the Church and the Bible, the God of "revelation." Indeed, it is not until late in the sixteenth century, in England with the Anglican "compromise" (between the authority-based Catholic Church and the Bible-based Calvinist Church), that we find natural theology—the Argument from Design particularly—starts to have a major place in its own right. The Book of Nature now takes equal place with the Book of Revelation—although note that this is as much for cultural as for theological reasons. The English needed an ideology, a religion, between the fanaticism of the Catholic hordes on the continent and the fanaticism of the Protestant hordes North of the Border (with Scotland).

This did not mean that the argument stood still. The scientific revolution of the sixteenth and seventeenth centuries expelled final causes from the physical sciences. No longer was the inorganic world a support of the argument to complexity. Francis Bacon

(1605), the great philosopher of the revolution, dismissed final causes as akin to Vestal Virgins—decorative but barren. René Descartes, the seventeenth-century French philosopher and mathematician, was no more enthusiastic. Yet in the biological sciences the complexity was undeniable. More so in fact after the microscope was developed and revealed the wonderful world of life beneath regular human sight. The physicist Robert Boyle particularly stressed that it is impossible to study nature without making reference to ends, to intentions, to values. "For there are some things in nature so curiously contrived, and so exquisitely fitted for certain operations and uses, that it seems little less than blindness in him, that acknowledges, with the Cartesians [the followers of Descartes], a most wise Author of things, not to conclude, that, though they may have been designed for other (and perhaps higher) uses, yet they were designed for this use."[7] In this he was followed by many others, notably John Ray the naturalist.

INFERENCE TO THE BEST EXPLANATION

We have an easy and direct passage down to William Paley, who was less an innovative thinker and more one with a great ability to take up the ideas of others and present them in a clear and convincing fashion. Except of course there was one major bump that Paley may have ignored but that was there nevertheless. This was the systematic attack that the philosophers were now directing against the argument. Most notably, we have David Hume's posthumously published *Dialogues Concerning Natural Religion* (1779). Hume took the Argument from Design to pieces and showed that it fails almost right down the line. Most particularly, Hume pointed out that rather than a single designer, it is far more reasonable to conclude that there is a squad of designers, and that our world is neither the first nor the last. Think of any reasonably efficient artifact that you like. Rarely if ever is it the work of one person, and even more rarely does it appear all at once entire. It usually takes years if not centuries of trial and effort, and is always open to improvement. Hume also pointed out that if indeed the product reflects the designer, then we might be wary of wanting to worship a god who brings about so much pain and misery. This is the traditional problem of evil, or the so-called theodicy problem. In a very eighteenth-century sort of way, Hume instanced the pain from gout and like diseases. Would a good and efficient designer have made humans liable to such ailments?

Why did people ignore Hume? For one very good reason, that even Hume himself acknowledged at the end of his *Dialogues*. It is all very well bashing God, but if not Him, then who? Intricate organized complexity like the eye and the hand does not just occur. It has to have a sufficient reason, and blind law is just not enough. As pointed out above, blind law leads to decay and mess. The mistake in assuming that Hume must have carried all before him is in thinking of the Argument from Design as a simple analogical argument. The eye is like a telescope. Telescopes have telescope designers. Therefore eyes have eye designers. The Great Optician in the Sky! Truly the Argument from Design is what philosophers call "an argument to the best explanation." If you have eliminated all of the rivals, the one that is left standing is your best bet. As Sherlock Holmes put it to his friend Dr. Watson, in Arthur Conan Doyle's *The Sign of the Four*: "How often have I told you that when you have eliminated the impossible, whatever remains, *however improbable*, must be the truth."

If the living world is complex, then there must be a God. This was the state of affairs at the beginning of the nineteenth century, and it was the father of comparative anatomy Georges Cuvier—incidentally, a Protestant even though he was French—who stressed the complexity of the living world. Following Aristotle he argued that final cause is the key to biological understanding.

> Natural history nevertheless has a rational principle that is exclusive to it and which it employs with great advantage on many occasions; it is the *conditions of existence* or, popularly, *final causes*. As nothing may exist which does not include the conditions which made its existence possible, the different parts of each

creature must be coordinated in such a way as to make possible the whole organism, not only in itself but in its relationship to those which surround it, and the analysis of these conditions often leads to general laws as well founded as those of calculation or experiment.[8]

In an argument that he almost certainly got from Immanuel Kant (in the *Third Critique*), Cuvier used the teleological aspect of organisms as a refutation of evolution. There can be no natural transition from one form to another because all intermediates would be literally neither fish nor fowl—they would be adapted neither for one station in life nor another station in life.

CHARLES DARWIN

Charles Robert Darwin (1809–1882), the English naturalist and father of evolutionary theory, was brought up on Paley and his early nineteenth-century successors, chiefly the authors of the so-called *Bridgewater Treatises*, a series of volumes, published during the 1830s, designed to show the workings of God in nature. For Darwin, final cause was always the biological problem to be solved. And it was to this that Darwin's mechanism of evolutionary change, natural selection, chiefly spoke. It was intended to explain things like the hand and the eye, things that are complex and yet as if designed. Things that he called "adaptations."

To pick up on the argument of the *Origin of Species*, published in 1859 (although in fact Darwin had discovered selection some twenty years earlier), first there is the Malthusian move to a struggle for existence.

A struggle for existence inevitably follows from the high rate at which all organic beings tend to increase. Every being, which during its natural lifetime produces several eggs or seeds, must suffer destruction during some period of its life, and during some season or occasional year, otherwise, on the principle of geometrical increase, its numbers would quickly become so inordinately great that no country could support the product. Hence, as more individuals are produced than can possibly survive, there must in every case be a struggle for existence, either one individual with another of the same species, or with the individuals of distinct species, or with the physical conditions of life. It is the doctrine of Malthus applied with manifold force to the whole animal and vegetable kingdoms; for in this case there can be no artificial increase of food, and no prudential restraint from marriage.[9]

Note that, more than a struggle for existence, Darwin had need of a struggle for reproduction. It is no good being built like a football player if your sexual interests are those of a philosopher. But, understanding the struggle in this way, and assuming ongoing naturally occurring variation, natural selection follows at once.

> Let it be borne in mind in what an endless number of strange peculiarities our domestic productions, and, in a lesser degree, those under nature, vary; and how strong the hereditary tendency is. Under domestication, it may be truly said that the whole organization becomes in some degree plastic. Let it be borne in mind how infinitely complex and close-fitting are the mutual relations of all organic beings to each other and to their physical conditions of life. Can it, then, be thought improbable, seeing that variations useful to man have undoubtedly occurred, that other variations useful in some way to each being in the great and complex battle of life, should sometimes occur in the course of thousands of generations? If such do occur, can we doubt (remembering that many more individuals are born than can possibly survive) that individuals having any advantage, however slight, over others, would have the best chance of surviving and of procreating their kind? On the other hand we may feel sure that any variation in the least degree injurious would be rigidly destroyed. This preservation of favourable variations and the rejection of injurious variations, I call Natural Selection.[10]

Natural selection speaks to final cause, to the complexity at the heart of the Argument from Design. In the light of this, let me make three points. First, if natural selection does what it is supposed to do, then it wrecks the Argument from Design. It does nothing to the first part of the argument. In fact, it reinforces it. Darwin agrees fully with the natural theologian—in fact, I would go so far as to say that agreement is the mark of the true Darwinian—that the truly significant aspect of the organic world is its end-directed complexity. This is the problem to be solved. The point is that the argument to the best explanation no longer points to God. There is the natural (that is, nontheological, nonsupernatural) alternative of natural selection. As Richard Dawkins has said rightly, after Darwin (and only after Darwin) is it possible to be an intellectually fulfilled atheist.

The second point is that although it may be possible to be an atheist, nothing so far has said that one must be an atheist. Richard Dawkins is an atheist. He writes:

> In a universe of blind physical forces and genetic replication, some people are going to get hurt, other people are going to get lucky, and you won't find any rhyme or reason in it, nor any justice. The universe we observe has precisely the properties we should expect if there is, at bottom, no design, no purpose, no evil and no good, nothing but blind, pitiless indifference. As that unhappy poet A. E. Houseman put it:
>> For Nature, heartless, witless Nature
>> Will neither know nor care.
> DNA neither knows nor cares. DNA just is. And we dance to its music.[11]

This may indeed all be so. The point is that you have got to argue to it. You cannot just assume it.

The third point is that Darwinism does lay itself open to rejection (or at least attempted rejection) on the design question, in the sense that because it emphasizes the design-like nature of the world, if one can refute natural selection or diminish its power, the Argument from Design is right back in business. If you were against the Design-Argument therefore, you might be tempted to another strategy, namely, trying to attack the first part of the argument, the argument to complexity. Suppose you say that the world is really not that complex and end-directed. Hence, natural selection is really not that needed. But hence also neither is God!

You might think that after two-and-a-half-thousand years of people accepting organic complexity, there is not much chance of its being rejected. Kant (1790) went so far as to say that one cannot even think about organisms without conceptualizing in terms of complexity. Life scientists

> say that nothing in such forms of life is in vain, and they put the maxim on the same footing of validity as the fundamental principle of all natural science, that nothing happens by chance. They are, in fact, quite as unable to free themselves from this teleological principle as from that of general physical science. For just as the abandonment of the latter would leave them without any experience at all, so the abandonment of the former would leave them with no clue to assist their observation of a type of natural things that have once come to be thought under the conception of physical ends.[12]

However, perhaps Kant was simply wrong about this. At least, sufficiently wrong that a designer seems less than pressing.

As it happens, by the time Darwin published the *Origin*, as he himself acknowledged, many biologists—including his own great supporter Thomas Henry Huxley—were arguing that the world is nothing like as design-like as often claimed. In particular, picking up on something which Aristotle had mentioned, many anatomists (above all, the nature philosophers or *Naturphilosophen* of early nineteenth-century Germany) stressed the nonadaptive isomorphisms between organisms, especially vertebrates. Huxley agreed that natural selection is working but he was never that impressed by adaptation—as a morphologist he found it rather inconvenient, because surface adaptations concealed what he thought were deeper nonadaptive connections between organisms. Darwin himself of course recognized this—unlike Cuvier (a nonevolutionist remember), who wanted to say that the isomorphisms (that we now call "homologies") are simply incidental by-products of final causes in different organisms, Darwin saw that homology is not directly adaptive, but obviously the result of shared descent. He called this "unity of type." But Darwin never thought of this as something that pushed adaptive complexity to the sidelines. Anything but:

> It is generally acknowledged that all organic beings have been formed on two great laws[:] Unity of Type, and the Conditions of Existence. By unity of type is meant that fundamental agreement in structure, which we see in organic beings of the same class, and which is quite independent of their habits of life. On my theory, unity of type is explained by unity of descent. The expression of conditions of existence, so often insisted on by the illustrious Cuvier, is fully embraced by the principle of natural selection. For natural selection acts by either now adapting the varying parts of each being to its organic and inorganic conditions of life; or by having adapted them during long-past periods of time: the adaptations being aided in some cases by use and disuse, being slightly affected by the direct action of the external conditions of life, and being in all cases subjected to the several laws of growth. Hence, in fact, the law of the Conditions of Existence is the higher law; as it includes, through the inheritance of former adaptations, that of Unity of Type.[13]

Notice also that natural selection is a process that works with what is at hand, modifying and multiplying, rather than creating anew. This is something that Darwin himself recognized fully. In his little book on orchids (published three years after the *Origin*), Darwin stressed that if something is needed, selection cannot simply design from scratch. It must work with the things available, and this will often lead to duplication and like phenomena, until the end product looks more like a Rube Goldberg (in England, Heath Robinson) contraption, than anything designed by an intelligent being.

> Although an organ may not have been originally formed for some special purpose, if it now serves for this end we are justified in saying that it is specially contrived for it. On the same principle, if a man were to make a *machine* for some special purpose, but were to use old wheels, springs, and pulleys, only slightly altered, the whole *machine*, with all its parts, might be said to be specially contrived for that purpose. Thus throughout nature almost every part of each living being has probably served, in a slightly modified condition, for diverse purposes, and has acted in the living *machinery* of many ancient and distinct specific forms.[14]

In other words, Darwin managed to turn the problematic nature of adaptation—that often it is just not as sensible as it should be—on its head, both as confirmation of selection and critique of the Argument from Design. Given natural selection as the causal mechanism, you expect adaptation often to be string and sealing wax. Given divine intelligence, you expect something better.

Later in life (under the influence of Huxley), Darwin became something of an agnostic. But you should understand that for Darwin keeping God out of science was a methodological matter rather than one of theology. At least through the writing of the *Origin* he was still prepared to accept some kind of designer, albeit one at a distance. To his American friend and supporter, the Harvard botanist Asa Gray, Darwin wrote: "I see no necessity in the belief that the eye was expressly designed. On the other hand I cannot anyhow be contented to view this wonderful universe & especially the nature of man, & to conclude that everything is the result of brute force. I am inclined to look at everything as resulting from designed laws, with the details, whether good or bad, left to the working out of what we may call chance."[15]

It is well known that after the *Origin of Species* was published, evolution was a smash hit success but selection was not.[16] The reasons for this are complex and not entirely scientific. Evolution fit with the spirit of the times—a lawbound account of origins, that (as everyone thought) led up to our own species. Selection, on the other hand, was problematic not only because in the absence of a decent theory of heredity it was hard to see how it could function efficiently, but also because it was the Huxley-vision that prevailed rather than the Darwin-vision. Complexity—adaptive complexity that is—was rather played down.

It is true that there were those who continued to insist on the complex nature of the organic world, and who continued to insist that selection could not do the job and that hence the God of Paley stands intact. One in England was Darwin's old mentor, the professor of geology at the University of Cambridge, Adam Sedgwick. He hated the *Origin* precisely because he thought it denied design. Another in America was the Calvinist, systematic theologian at Princeton Theological Seminary, Charles Hodge. He asked: *What is Darwinism?* Back came the stern reply: *It is Atheism.* Even Asa Gray, although an evolutionist, felt that selection could not explain design, something he (as an evangelical Presbyterian) fervently accepted. However, generally, complementing the lack of enthusiasm of biologists for adaptive complexity, as the nineteenth century drew to a close, we see a corresponding lack of enthusiasm by theologians for the traditional Argument from Design. Newman was not alone.

People now tended to see the teleology of the organic world as lying in the historical process rather than in the individual organism—I mean, people saw a kind of progressivist sweep to humankind in evolution's history and this was taken as the new proof of God, inasmuch as one is still seeking a proof. Thus, the Reverend Henry Ward Beecher, brother of the novelist, charismatic preacher, notorious adulterer: "If single acts would evince design, how much more a vast universe, that by inherent laws gradually builded itself, and then created its own plants and animals, a universe so adjusted that it left by the way the poorest things, and steadily wrought toward more complex, ingenious, and beautiful results!" Continuing: "Who designed this mighty machine, created matter, gave to it its laws, and impressed upon it that tendency which has brought forth the almost infinite results on the globe, and wrought them into a perfect system? Design by wholesale is grander than design by retail." Similar sentiments can be found in the writings of others, notably Frederick Temple, future Archbishop of Canterbury: "the world itself, by the perfect order of its changes and motions, and by the great beauty of all things visible, proclaims by a kind of silent testimony of its own both that it has been created, and also that it could not have been made other than by a God ineffable and invisible in greatness, and ineffable and invisible in beauty."[17]

AFTER DARWIN: THE TWENTIETH CENTURY

Moving into the twentieth century, in the realm of science the big event was the realization that Darwin was right about natural selection—it is a powerful mechanism, it does cause evolution, it does bring complexity into being. The 1930s and 1940s saw the melding of Darwinian selection with Mendelian (later molecular) genetics to make a fully functioning paradigm, neo-Darwinism (as the English tended to call it) or the synthetic theory of evolution (as the Americans called it). By the 1950s, natural selection rode supreme, thanks to studies on snails, on butterflies and moths, on fruit flies, and on many other organisms including plants.

This is the position that has remained dominant down to the present. It is true that selection has its biological critics. Stephen Jay Gould was persistent in his attacks on what he called panselectionism, seeing too much selection everywhere. Well known is his critique, coauthored by Richard Lewontin: "The Spandrels of San Marco." They argued strongly that evolutionists—Darwinians particularly—assume far too readily that living nature is adaptive, that it is functional. They did not want to deny that the hand and the eye are adaptations, for clearly they are. However, Gould and Lewontin felt that too often evolutionists think that every last organic feature has to be functional, the product of natural selection. Referring to the Leibnizian philosopher in Voltaire's *Candide,* they accused evolutionists of Panglossianism, thinking that these must be the best of all possible features in the best of all possible worlds. Supposedly, evolutionists invent "just so" stories—thus named from Rudyard Kipling's fantasy stories—with natural selection scenarios leading to adaptation.

As an alternative picture, Gould and Lewontin drew attention to the triangular decorative aspects of the tops of pillars in medieval churches. They argued that although such "spandrels" seem adaptive, they are just by-products of the builders' methods of keeping the roof in place. "The design is so elaborate, harmonious, and purposeful that we are tempted to view it as the starting point of any analysis, as the cause in some sense of the surrounding architecture." This, however, is to get things precisely backwards. "The system begins with an architectural constraint: the necessary four spandrels and their tapering triangular form. They provide a space in which the mosaicist worked; they set the quadripartite symmetry of the dome above."[18] Perhaps, argued Gould and Lewontin, we have a similar situation in the living world. Much that we think adaptive is merely a spandrel, and such things as constraints on development prevent anything like an optimally designed world. Perhaps things are much more random and haphazard—nonfunctional— than the Darwinian thinks possible.

Much ink has been spilt on this particular argument. The main point is that from our perspective these critics certainly give no help to the would-be invigorator of the Argument from Design. On the one hand, Gould and Lewontin do not deny adaptation or the role of natural selection. On the other hand, inasmuch as the living world is a hodgepodge of by-products and constraints and so forth, it is hardly a testament to the God of the Christians. So there is certainly no succor for traditional natural theology in this corner. Nor do we find much succor from the more orthodox Darwinians. It has already been pointed out that because Darwin makes it possible to be an intellectually fulfilled atheist, it does not follow that one should or must be an intellectually fulfilled atheist. However, from Darwin (who was not in fact an atheist) to Dawkins (who is very much an atheist) there has always been one major, evolution-based argument used to derive a non-God conclusion. This is the traditional problem of evil—a good, all-powerful God would not allow evil—brought up to date by reference to the cruel nature of the Darwinian process.

Could a Christian God have created, using the struggle for existence? In another passage from a letter quoted earlier (to Asa Gray, where he admitted that he thought that there was some sort of deity), Darwin made his worries very clear.

> With respect to the theological view of the question; this is always painful to me.—I am bewildered.—I had no intention to write atheistically. But I own that I cannot see, as plainly as others do, & as I sh^D. wish to do, evidence of design & beneficence on all sides of us. There seems to me too much misery in the world. I cannot persuade myself that a beneficent & omnipotent God would have designedly created the Ichneumonidae with the express intention of their feeding within the living bodies of caterpillars, or that a cat should play with mice. Not believing this, I see no necessity in the belief that the eye was expressly designed.[19]

Commenting on this passage, Dawkins writes:

> Actually Darwin's gradual loss of faith, which he downplayed for fear of upsetting his devout wife Emma, had more complex causes. His reference to the Ichneumonidae was aphoristic. The macabre habits to which he referred are shared by their cousins the digger wasps . . . A female digger wasp not only lays her egg in a caterpillar (or grasshopper or bee) so that her larva can feed on it but, according to Fabre and others, she carefully guides her sting into each ganglion of the prey's central nervous system, so

as to paralyze it *but not kill it*. This way, the meat keeps fresh. It is not known whether the paralysis acts as a general anesthetic, or if it is like curare in just freezing the victim's ability to move. If the latter, the prey might be aware of being eaten alive from inside but unable to move a muscle to do anything about it. This sounds savagely cruel but as we shall see, nature is not cruel, only pitilessly indifferent. This is one of the hardest lessons for humans to learn. We cannot admit that things might be neither good nor evil, neither cruel nor kind but simply callous—indifferent to all suffering, lacking all purpose.[20]

As it happens, I myself am not sure that this argument is quite as strong as the evolutionists think, but the point here is that by and large, although Dawkins may be extreme, he does speak for many. There would be agreement that there simply is no place for a designer.

Today's Christians have a slightly more complex position than the biologists, but although they obviously are not going to agree with the atheists, they are by no means entirely opposed to the atheists' thinking. In the first part of the twentieth century, natural theology generally came under very severe attack from Protestant theologians. Karl Barth particularly argued—in a strain that goes back to Martin Luther and was strongly represented in the nineteenth century by the Danish theologian Søren Kierkegaard—that natural theology is all wrong. Worse than wrong. It destroys faith. Unless one believes in the absurd—not the ridiculous but the nonjustifiable by reason—one is no true believer. If faith can be justified it can no longer be faith. Hence the Argument from Design is not only not wanted, it is positively destructive to the Christian's thinking. (Officially, whatever Newman may have said, to this day Catholic philosophy insists that Aquinas was right and the arguments work. Unofficially, many Catholic philosophers and theologians think the Protestants may have a point.)

Much debate and much criticism followed the enunciation of this stark doctrine. Not a few pointed out that Barth—who wanted to base much of his thinking on the Bible (not the literal Bible of American evangelicals)—was not entirely consistent in his own position. Although the Bible as a whole is certainly not a work of natural theology, there are elements of such thinking in Saint Paul (who was educated in Greek philosophy) and even hints in the Old Testament. "The heavens declare the glory of God; and the firmament sheweth his handy-work" (Psalms 19:1). More importantly, people after Barth feel that he was too severe in his rejection. It is true that natural theology traditionally conceived—reason leading to knowledge of the existence and nature of the Godhead—no longer works, but this is not to say that nature has no significance for the believer. This is very much the position of Barth's sometime student, the German theologian Wolfhart Pannenberg. He urges us to embrace a theology of nature rather than a natural theology. Like Newman, he feels that the believer responds to God's creation seeing it illuminated by the realization that God exists and is good, rather than looking for proof of God in nature.

> If the god of the Bible is the creator of the universe, then it is not possible to understand fully or even appropriately the processes of nature without any reference to that God. If, on the contrary, nature can be appropriately understood without reference to the God of the Bible, then that God cannot be the creator of the universe, and consequently he cannot be truly God and be trusted as a source of moral teaching either.

Science has its job and religion its job: "abstract knowledge of regularities should not claim full and exclusive competence regarding the explanation of nature; if it does so, the reality of God is denied by implication."[21]

ENTER INTELLIGENT DESIGN

The late Langdon Gilkey, probably the most eminent American theologian in the second half of the twentieth century, used to joke that when his colleagues in the medical school ribbed him about holding old-fashioned notions, he would respond by asking about their Department of Bleeding. When they replied indignantly that bleeding was a long-outmoded practice, he would counter that theology moves on just like any other human subject. Because people held sincerely to one set of beliefs in one earlier century, we should not thereby assume that we must necessarily hold to just those beliefs in our century.

We have certainly seen the truth of this in natural theology, most particularly in the case of the Argument from Design. It was a good argument and much good science and theology was done because of it. But its heyday is now past, and inasmuch as it still has force it is in different ways and directions. Far from being a cause for regret, this is what makes life interesting, and for the Christian is the true proof that we are not just modified monkeys but made in the image of God. However, in America today there is an attempt to put back the clock and to restore the Argument from Design to its past position of influence and glory. This is the aim of the Intelligent Design movement.

I will say little about ID in this essay because others in the volume will be dealing with it in far more detail. All I want to do in concluding my essay is to stress that ID is not new. We have seen it all before. The ID enthusiast Michael Behe, author of *Darwin's Black Box*, is almost Paley word for word. He claims that the world is so intricate—irreducible complexity—that it cannot be explained by blind law, and certainly not by natural selection. Hence there must be a designer. Although Behe and his fellows tend to be cagey about this, we know full well that this designer is no natural phenomenon. It is the God of the Christian.

Of course the ID movement puts the old wine in new bottles. There is much talk about complexity at the biochemical level. There is (especially from the mathematician and philosopher of science William Dembski) much talk about theoretical criteria for design-like phenomena. But essentially, it is the argument of Plato, of Aquinas, and of Paley. There is nothing to be ashamed of in this, but there is nothing to be excited about this either. When Behe suggests (as he does) that he is authoring a breakthrough of the magnitude of Copernicus and heliocentrism, he is not just embarrassing, he is historically wrong. Been there already. Done that already.

So in conclusion I urge that people not approach the ID movement as if it were some altogether new set of ideas or approach. It may be that you will conclude that it does have something new that commands attention. But before you come to such a conclusion, put it in historical context and ask why it is that although the Argument from Design once had power, for so many—believers as well as nonbelievers—this power is now gone. It could just be that the ID supporters are ignoring the findings and deep thinking that has brought others to their point of skepticism. There is no good reason why you too should ignore these findings and deep thinking.

The Aerodynamics of Flying Carpets

Why Biologists Are Loath to "Teach the Controversy"

SCOTT F. GILBERT and the Swarthmore College Evolution and Development Seminar

These are the notes of a person who majored in both biology and religion and who has profound respect for both. I believe Alfred North Whitehead's dictum that science and religion are two of the most important forces on this planet and that our future largely depends on how these two great forces interact.[1] I see Intelligent Design as a particularly impoverished and dishonest interaction between these two critically important forces.

When I "teach the controversy" to my undergraduates, I do so because it falls into the general pedagogical principle used by geneticists and medical educators: if you want to know what's normal, find the loss-of-function mutant. Imagine science if there were neither controlled experiments nor any demand for materialistic causation. The result would be something like Intelligent Design. I remind the students that science is very good at paring away what is improbable, leaving the probable to be further tested. Indeed, if "recognizing excellence wherever it may be" is one definition of the liberal arts curriculum, I believe that "recognizing nonsense no matter how well it is packaged" is a chief duty of its science curriculum. Even before Intelligent Design, I assigned students to read creationist literature, especially Duane Gish's *Evolution: The Fossils Say No!*, and find the evidence for or against Gish's assertions. They were amazed to find the scientific and logical errors in his narrative against evolution, the lack of evidence for the creationist views, and the prevalence of scientific evidence against his views. I find that this is a useful lesson to teach students. In this age of professionally packaged websites, nonsense has never looked better. I am not alone in this judgment that Intelligent Design is well-packaged nonsense. Every course that "teaches the controversy" should have in its syllabus Judge John E. Jones's 2005 decision in the *Kitzmiller v. Dover Area School District* (as well as the "Wedge Strategy" document from the Discovery Institute).

When I teach evolutionary developmental biology, I try to incorporate this material into laboratory discussions; but I discuss it as sociology, not as science. Indeed, when I was asked to write this article, I gave this assignment to my students in my evolutionary developmental biology seminar as their final exam. The scientific portions of this essay are their work. I teach the controversy, then, because it illustrates several critical features of good scientific practice. As a loss-of-function mutant, ID provides an "experiment" that helps me teach students what science might be if it lost its respect for evidence and controls.

WHEN THERE IS NO "THERE" THERE

My field of science, evolutionary developmental biology, is a crucial one for the debate. Design proponents sometimes use it to create the illusion of a rift over evolution within the scientific community. For instance, Intelligent Design advocate Jonathan Wells claims that I and several other evolutionary developmental biologists are against natural selection. He also says, "These people *hate* it when I quote them; but these are their words, not mine."[2] Actually, I usually don't mind it at all when he quotes me. For I can use his quotations of me as examples of the "breathtaking inanity"[3] of Intelligent Design "scholarship." Since I've published several papers arguing that

Charles Darwin recognized the importance of the embryological approach to evolution, Wells's calling me an antievolutionist is as absurd as my calling George W. Bush an ecofeminist. So I really don't get angry when I read these remarks.

However, this comment of Wells exposes two notions dear to Intelligent Design proponents. First, they believe that any evidence against what textbooks say evolution is constitutes a victory for Intelligent Design. If evolutionists (or at least those whose ideas get into the textbooks) are wrong, then ID is right. Of course, the followers of the Flying Spaghetti Monster (FSM) know better. The FSM pseudoreligion was invented by Robert Henderson, an engineer who felt that if the Kansas school board should allow nonmaterialistic explanations to be taught in science classes, then the creation of the world by the FSM is as good a story as any other (see www .venganza.org). Second, Wells's comments show that any criticism about the *mechanisms* of evolution, such as those made by evolutionary developmental biologists, will be held up as evidence against evolution itself. The actual argument made by evolutionary developmental biologists is that current evolutionary explanations are incomplete without adding developmental genetics to the current approach wherein population genetics predominates. We have no problems with natural selection or descent with modification; we want to add developmental biology as a way to provide mechanisms for producing those variants that nature will select. For example, Cynthia Hughes and Thomas Kaufman argue that when confronted with the question of how specific modifications of the arthropod body arose, "to answer by invoking natural selection is correct—but incomplete. The fangs of a centipede . . . and the claws of a lobster accord these organisms a fitness advantage. However, the crux of the mystery is this: From what developmental genetic changes did these novelties arise in the first place."[4]

Evolutionary developmental biologists are looking at the steps prior to natural selection, and our paradigm is that evolution is caused by heritable changes in development between generations. Thus, when we say that the contemporary one-toed horse had a five-toed ancestor, we are saying that this part of equine evolution was caused by changes in the placement of cartilage cells during embryogenesis. So even though evolutionary developmental biologists claim that natural selection is incomplete, we are definitely within the framework of Darwin. As I have argued, by combining developmental genetics with population genetics, "we are still approaching evolution in the two ways that Darwin recognized."[5] This is in no conceivable way an antievolutionary (or even an anti-Darwinian) standpoint. To argue that it is, as the Intelligent Design advocates do, is to deliberately misconstrue our experiments and explanations. It is rhetoric, not serious inquiry or debate.

And while trying (by misconstruing evolution) to declare evolution wrong, Intelligent Design proponents have no alternative naturalistic theory with which to replace it. Thus, most biologists would probably claim that there is no controversy. You can only have a scientific controversy when there are at least two opposing scientific positions. The debate between evolutionary biology and Intelligent Design is like a debate over whether the aerodynamics of the Boeing 747 are superior to those of flying carpets. So the first reason why many scientists don't want to teach the controversy is because there isn't a scientific controversy. There are plenty of active and interesting scientific controversies within evolutionary biology—are birds feathered dinosaurs? how did land vertebrates evolve lungs? what animal is the ancestor of turtles?—and these controversies have scientists arguing different positions based on their interpretations of data. But Intelligent Design is not science. It's not even bad science. Intelligent Design is antiscience, an active denial that science can explain the natural world through nonteleological and nonsupernatural processes. The world (in the words of the Intelligent Design proponents) is "irreducibly complex."

There is nothing scientific to counter in such debates. ID proponents have not put forth a testable alternative to evolution. Nor is there any Intelligent Design program that serves as a counterpoint against evolutionary biology. ID has no program to discover anything. The following quotation is from the transcript of the Intelligent Design trial in Dover, Pennsylvania. Here, one of the major proponents of the ID movement, biochemist Michael Behe,[6] is being questioned by attorney Eric Rothschild:

Q: Please describe the mechanism that intelligent design proposes for how complex biological structures arose.

A: Well, the word "mechanism" can be used in many ways . . . When I was referring to intelligent design, I meant that we can perceive that in the process by which a complex biological structure arose, we can infer that intelligence was involved. . . .

Q: What is the mechanism that intelligent design proposes?

A: And I wonder, could—am I permitted to know what I replied to your question the first time?

Q: I don't think I got a reply, so I'm asking you. You've made this claim here [reading], "Intelligent design theory focuses exclusively on the proposed mechanism of how complex biological structures arose." And I want to know, what is the mechanism that intelligent design proposes for how complex biological structures arose?

A: Again, it does not propose a mechanism in the sense of a step-by-step description of how those structures arose. But it can infer that in the mechanism, in the process by which these structures arose, an intelligent cause was involved.[7]

The text goes on and on. There is no science in Intelligent Design. Intelligent Design advocates propose no mechanisms to explain biodiversity. There is no substance to Intelligent Design.

The second reason most biologists are loath to "teach the controversy" is that Intelligent Design has no respect for evidence. Scientists just can't make things up. If a hypothesis is shown to be false, it must be retracted or its proponents must demonstrate that the criticism is not conclusive. This is not the case for Intelligent Design. I'll again use the works of Michael Behe as an example, since he is one of the few scientists who is in this movement (especially if you exclude people like me who are listed as anti-Darwinian). Behe's book *Darwin's Black Box* (1996) makes certain declarative statements about nature and about scientists' ignorance concerning how bacterial flagella and the vertebrate eye could have possibly evolved. Each one of these assertions has been falsified, and people like Brown University biologist Kenneth Miller have repeatedly and publicly criticized Behe's work for being scientifically wrong.[8] Scientists actually know a lot about the things that Behe claims we don't know anything about. For instance, Behe states emphatically that the bacterial flagellum is so remarkably constructed that its component parts could not have evolved for separate functions. They would all have had to evolve concurrently, and this would indicate an "end," since they would have no function individually. Biologists have excellent evidence that the components of the bacterial flagellum actually had a separate function, and in some bacteria, they still perform these ancestral functions. Similarly, Behe claims that the component proteins of the complement cascade of the human immune system are so perfectly integrated that these component parts could not have existed separately and if you remove any one of them, the system falls apart. Yet, scientists have known for years that the complement system is a jerry-rigged amalgamation of proteins that have had separate functions elsewhere, and that there are several organisms that have fully functional complement cascades despite lacking one or more of these parts.

One of the basic principles of scientific evidence is that if you make a statement and it is subsequently proven wrong, you retract it. Such has not been done;[9] Behe's refusal to consider the enormous amount of evidence that refutes his claims makes it difficult for biologists to take him seriously.

Behe is not the only Intelligent Design "scientist" who ignores or distorts scientific evidence. The Reverend Jonathan Wells, who has a Ph.D. in developmental biology, has on his website a remarkable experiment that he claims disproves the notion that genes had anything to do with development and the formation of bodily structures. According to his website:

My experiments focused on a reorganization of the egg cytoplasm after fertilization which causes the embryo to elongate into a tadpole; if I blocked the reorganization, the result was a ball of belly cells; if I induced a second reorganization after the first, I could produce a two-headed tadpole. Yet this reorganization had nothing to do with the egg's DNA, and proceeded quite well even in its absence (though the embryo eventually needed its DNA to supply it with additional proteins). So DNA does not program the development of the embryo.[10]

I received several emails about this, especially from philosophers. Can this possibly be true? Yes, the experiments are described correctly; and the interpretation would be hilarious were it not for its propaganda value. The explanation for this is simple, but not obvious to the person who hasn't had biological training. Here's the trick: the early development in the frog doesn't have a thing to do with the nuclear genome. In the species he was using, the nuclear genome isn't even active until the twelfth cell division. Rather, the early development of the frog has to do with its mother's genome! The mother's genes, active in the oocyte, encode the protein β-catenin. The localization of this protein is the first step in forming the head. If you disrupt it during the first division, no head will form; if you put it in a second region of the egg toward the end of the first division, two heads will form. Voilà. Certainly there is no absence of scientific knowledge here; nor is there any hint of Intelligent Design; just good old-fashioned genes working in the oocyte as they have been known to work since the geneticist Alfred Sturtevant first proposed maternal effect genes in 1923.[11]

Does Wells know about these data relating maternal β-catenin to head formation in the frog? I think he does: he was a coauthor of the paper that helped discover its role. In this paper, "Microtubule-Mediated Transport of Organelles and Localization of β-Catenin to the Future Dorsal Side of *Xenopus* Eggs," Wells and his colleagues write:

A second axis also can be produced by taking cytoplasm from the vegetal pole before rotation (or from the equator on the prospective dorsal side after rotation) and injecting it into the ventral equatorial region of an egg that otherwise would form only one axis . . . We focused on β-catenin, a downstream protein of this pathway, because it has been shown to be both necessary and sufficient for the formation of dorsoanterior [head] structures.[12]

So I think we can conclude that Wells knows all about this material. However, by ignoring his own data, he can tell the public a convincing story that genes do not play a role in development (and hence, in evolution).[13] This is why I see Intelligent Design to be in the tradition of American flimflam artistry rather than the tradition of Plato, Saint Thomas Aquinas, and the Reverend Paley.

Third, Intelligent Design celebrates ignorance. ID proponents have claimed that they are in a long tradition that goes back to natural theology. Natural theology is a critically important philosophical and religious position, and it was one of the founding motivations for doing science. Reading a textbook such as Rev. William Kirby's *On the Power, Wisdom and Goodness of God as Manifested in the Creation of Animals and in Their History, Habits and Instincts* (*Bridgewater Treatise* 7; 1836) is to read good science based on careful observations. However, it differs from today's science in giving an Aristotelian Final Cause for these adaptations. Thus, one will find in Kirby a detailed analysis of the bird feather, ending with a paean to the Creator who made such feathers so that each bird would survive in its habitat and so that mankind might see and enjoy such beauty. In natural theology, the more detailed the science, the greater glory to the Creator. Natural theology did not fear science: indeed it helped create science. Isaac Newton, Robert Boyle, and other members of the Royal Society of London were prominent natural theologians. Intelligent Design, on the other hand, denies the ability of science to acquire knowledge about how the natural world arose. Duane Gish, the leader of the creation science movement that was the direct predecessor to Intelligent Design, said it very succinctly, "We do not know how God created, what processes he used, *for God used processes which are not now operating anywhere in the natural universe.* This is why we refer to divine creation as special creation. We cannot discover by scientific investigations anything about the creative processes used by God" (Gish's italics). As Robert Root-Bernstein has noted, while natural theology was a goad and motivation for discovery, Intelligent Design pronounces ignorance as our wisdom.[14]

Having established ignorance of the natural world as our proper attitude, Intelligent Design advocates would place science on the same level as superstition. For example, in his testimony at the Dover trial, Michael Behe remarked that the notion of science espoused by Intelligent Design proponents would allow astrology to also be taught in science classes. As Judge Jones summarized it in his decision:

> ID is predicated on supernatural causation, as we previously explained and as various expert testimony revealed. (17:96 (Padian); 2:35–36 (Miller); 14:62 (Alters)). ID takes a natural phenomenon and, instead of accepting or seeking a natural explanation, argues that the explanation is supernatural. (5:107 (Pennock)). Further support for the conclusion that ID is predicated on supernatural causation is found in the ID reference book to which ninth grade biology students are directed, *Pandas*. *Pandas* states, in pertinent part, as follows: "Darwinists object to the view of intelligent design *because it does not give a natural cause explanation* of how the various forms of life started in the first place. Intelligent design means that various forms of life began abruptly, through an intelligent agency, with their distinctive features already intact—fish with fins and scales, birds with feathers, beaks, and wings, etc." P-11 at 99–100 (emphasis added). Stated another way, ID posits that animals did not evolve naturally through evolutionary means but were created abruptly by a non-natural, or supernatural, designer . . . Professor Fuller agreed that ID aspires to "change the ground rules" of science and lead defense expert Professor Behe admitted that his broad-

ened definition of science, which encompasses ID, would also embrace astrology. (28:26 (Fuller); 21:37–42 (Behe)).[15]

Ignorance of the natural world is dangerous; Intelligent Design proponents advocate this pernicious condition.

The fourth reason biologists do not generally wish to teach the controversy is that ID requires unwarranted and unscientific assumptions. Some of Intelligent Design's most powerful arguments depend on a simple fallacy: the assumption of an end point, a *telos*. William Dembski, for instance, will claim that it is impossible to evolve a particular protein because it has 100 amino acids and the chance of this occurring randomly is 1 in 20^{100} since there can be any one of 20 amino acids in any position. Multiply that by all the proteins in the body and one can see that the body is indeed impossible. But such supporters of ID don't know a billionth of how impossible it is! Let's say that your mother ovulated 500 eggs during her life and that your father produced 2×10^{12} sperm. The chances of *you* being born, then, are 1 in 10^{15}. Now the chance that your father is who he is also is about 1 in 10^{15}, as is the chance of your specific mother being born. So the chances of your grandparents giving rise to you is 1 in 10^{45}. Another reason not to argue with the Intelligent Design people, then, is that, by their own logic, they cannot exist (though of course neither can I).

The fallacy behind their statistics is the assumed end point. Evolution does not have an end point. The chances of *someone* being born from the union of your mother and father are rather high. The probability that the person will be someone with your particular genotype is astronomically low. Similarly, evolution does not care what the sequence of a protein is as long as it does its function. In some species, a particular protein is a metabolic enzyme in the liver. In other species, the same protein can be used as a structural protein in the lens to focus light upon the retina. Some species of fly use a protein called Bicoid to specify that the part of the embryo closest to the nurse cells becomes the head. In other flies, a protein called Hunchback will do the same job equally well. If one deletes the β-galactosidase gene in bacteria, the bacteria will die if fed only lactose sugar. However, if you first mutate these bacteria, some of them will gain the ability to metabolize lactose and will survive on the all-lactose diet. It turns out that some mutated enzymes will show a small ability to metabolize lactose.[16] Within a few generations of selection, the bacteria can thrive on lactose. The enzymes have a different sequence than the original β-galactosidase that had been deleted. But they did the job.

Because of such supposed improbability, Dembski claims that "there are natural systems that cannot be adequately explained in terms of undirected natural forces and that exhibit features which in any other circumstance we would attribute to intelligence."[17] Actually, scientists have been able to explain these natural systems very well and supernatural forces need not apply. Indeed, when non-natural explanations are allowed to be considered in scientific discussions, no amount of negative evidence will sway believers. Bad math, the lack of respect for evidence, the inculcation of ignorance, and the desire to include nonnatural explanations for natural phenomena are the four horsemen who bring death to scientific inquiry. Who can blame biologists for not wanting to teach them?

A LOUSY MUNICIPAL ENGINEER

Three engineers were arguing about what type of engineer God is. The first, pointing to our ability to walk, talk, swallow, and type claimed that God must be a *mechanical* engineer of the highest order. The second engineer countered, "That's child's play compared to the central nervous system." Invoking our capacities for cognition, memory, and emotion, he proposed that God must be the archetypal *electrical* engineer. The third engineer shook his head, and said, "No, God is a *municipal* engineer, and not a very good one." The other enineers were shocked. "How could you say this?" they demanded. The third engineer looked at them and answered. "Who but a lousy municipal engineer would put a toxic waste disposal duct through prime recreation area?"

This joke—much beloved by renal developmental biologists—gets close to the nub of the matter. First, biologists don't see God as an engineer, nor do they see evolution as an engineer. If evolution is to be personified, François Jacob has pointed out that evolution is then a bricoleur, a tinkerer.[18] Second, the science underlying the joke is important for understanding one of the most valuable lessons developmental biology teaches about evolution: organogenesis is codevelopment. For instance, the reason that the urinary waste duct goes through prime recreation area is that the gonads and the kidneys arise from the same original group of cells (the intermediate mesoderm) and that these cells induce each other's existence. The testis, for instance, cannot form without the kidney tube entering it. Which is a good thing, because the kidney tube in males becomes modified to get the sperm out of the testes! That is why men have the same opening for sperm and urine. Evolution is a tinkerer, and if there's a spare tube available, it can use it for some new function. And third, integrating the urinary system with the genital system is not good engineering strategy. It's a patched-together compromise. My wife is a gynecologist who has to deal with these design flaws on a daily basis. Her critique of Intelligent Design harks back to Darwin's writing Asa Gray (mentioned in chapter 2) that an omniscient and benevolent deity would not have made such a poorly designed world. When she saw the *New York Times* article showing all the men of the Orwellian-named "Discovery Institute," she asked if any *woman* believed that silliness.

Evolution's tinkering can explain many other anatomical relationships that would be considered poor engineering. The vagus ("wanderer") nerve is well named, since it wanders from the head, down into the neck, through the thorax, and into the abdomen, where it innervates the heart and the smooth muscle of the intestine. While in the thorax, it splits into a branch that loops around the aorta and runs back up the neck in the opposite direction from whence it came before it reaches the voice box. What is inexplicable in design terms makes sense in the light of our evolutionary ancestry. Fishes have hearts and vagus nerves but lack necks—the heart is situated between the gills underneath the back of the head. The vagus nerve and its branches once had a direct course, but in the development of land-living vertebrates, the neck developed, the heart was pushed into the thorax, and the vagus nerve was stretched out into a loop in the process.[19]

Although the kidney and gonads are remarkably complex and fascinating organs, the eye is the paradigmatic example of Paley's watch, the classic example of that-which-cannot-be-evolved. Proponents of Intelligent Design often cite the eye as a prime example of a biological structure that is too complex to have evolved: because the eye's parts must be arranged perfectly in order for it to provide vision, natural selection supposedly would not favor the less complex, transitional forms of the eye, nor would it have favored the individual parts of an eye. In other words, because the eye does not function when even one of its parts is removed, a simpler eye could never have been useful to its owner and therefore could never have evolved. Since natural selection could not plausibly drive the evolution of the eye, it must have been designed. Behe has declared the eye "irreducibly complex":

> By *irreducibly complex* I mean a single system composed of several well-matched, interacting parts that contribute to the basic function, wherein the removal of any one of the parts causes the system to effectively cease functioning.

Behe goes on to elaborate,

> An irreducibly complex system cannot be produced directly (that is, by continuously improving the initial function, which continues to work by the same mechanism) by slight, successive modifications of a precursor system because any precursor to an irreducibly complex system that is missing a part is by definition nonfunctional.[20]

The vertebrate eye is indeed a complex structure. In the standard description of the adult eye, light is transmitted through a transparent cornea and focused by the lens to form an image on the neural retina. Eye function depends on this arrangement of its parts. Notice that we define the eye by its adult structure and function. We have decided that the eye, consisting of the cornea, lens, and retina, with the function of being able to transmit two-dimensional images of real objects to the brain, is the system. This is a labeling system based on how humans perceive the function of the adult eye. It is not, however, a good reflection of how the eye develops within an organism nor how eyes evolved into different forms over time.

Evolution does not define systems, parts, or functions in human terms, nor does evolution occur with an end product in mind. Developmental biology shifts our focus from the apparent adult end point to the embryonic starting points. Thus, although it may be anatomically convenient to talk about the "parts" of the eye, these parts are not in fact intrinsically isolated from one another as they develop. The construction of the eye during early development occurs through a process of close interactions between adjacent layers of cells with different histories and properties, each causing the others to change their shape, growth rate, or type. These juxtaposed tissues produce signaling molecules that change the differentiation of the other tissue. Through such mechanisms, each part of the eye develops in conjunction with, not independently from, the parts around it. The process of reciprocal induction is found in many different developmental systems, and is also useful for explaining how tissues with very specific functions (such as the lens) can arise from tissues that have relatively nonspecific functions (such as the ectoderm, the outermost layer of an embryo).

In the early embryo, the signaling molecules that initiate eye development originate in the prospective neural plate, the tissue that will give rise to the brain and nervous system of the head. The neural plate receives signals from tissue that lies directly beneath it, causing it to extend outwards toward the surface ectoderm and form an optic vesicle. This optic vesicle is a convex bulge extending from the incipient brain and lying just underneath the ectoderm of the head. The head ectoderm (which would otherwise form epidermis) then responds to signals from the optic vesicle by producing a lens placode, which is a flat "plate" of several layers of lens-forming cells. However, only the head ectoderm region is competent to respond to the signals emitted by the optic vesicle. If the optic vesicle of a frog is placed underneath the ectoderm of the flank or abdomen, for instance, no lens tissue will form.

Once this lens placode has formed through the signals sent from the optic vesicle, it reciprocates by inducing the optic vesicle to become cup-shaped and to differentiate into retinal tissues. The retinal tissues, as they are forming, send signals that tell the lens placode to make lens cells and to invaginate into the head. Thus, the lens helps cause the formation of the retina, and the retina helps cause the formation of the lens. They form together. *Moreover*, as the developing lens enters the head, it produces factors that tell the ectodermal cells above them that they are to become the transparent cornea. Thus, the eye develops through reciprocal interactions between its multiple, tightly integrated parts. Once the neural ectoderm begins to move toward any competent head ectoderm, the formation of all the "parts" of the adult eye has already begun. This chain of signals causes the specified tissues of the retina, lens, and cornea to form in the proper arrangement, from what are initially unspecified tissues.

Thus, by no means does each part of the individual eye form in isolation and then "find" the other parts to fit together into the eye. The developing eye, as a unit, gives rise to the later, more complex adult eye through further inductive interactions. Furthermore, the mechanisms by which cell fate specification occur did not evolve *de novo* for the eye. These mechanisms, as we will soon see, have been around for much longer than has even the most basic eye structure.

The functional concept of an eye—a sensory organ for processing information received in the form of light—is found in all sorts of organisms from the most basic to the most highly derived. Yet despite the underlying functional similarity of light-receiving organs throughout the animal kingdom, the anatomical structures of these different eyes have made it difficult to infer a single common ancestry. Darwin and many of his successors pointed out that it is possible to trace a progressive increase in the complexity of light-sensing organs through the course of evolutionary history; in primitive organisms made of relatively few cells, a photosensitive cell could provide information as to whether it was day or night, and help them to orient themselves in the water. Slightly more derived forms of this system no larger than two cells in size—one photoreceptor cell and one pigmented cell that partially surrounded the photoreceptor— have been found in some cnidarians, the basal group of organisms that includes jellyfish, anemones, and coral.[21] This basic eye structure seems to have undergone divergent trajectories of increasing complexity through evolutionary time. Yet despite this broad trend, the fundamental structural and molecular differences between, for example, the fruit fly's compound eye and the human eye, have made it difficult for many to accept the idea of common ancestry.

But behind the different structures of all of these modern eyes one finds a particularly elegant piece of evidence for their descent with modification from a common photoreceptive ancestor. Despite the wide diversity of eye morphologies found throughout the animal kingdom, every eye appears to have developed according to instructions established by the gene encoding the Pax6 protein. Even in the ancestral two-celled prototypical eye, a protein very similar to Pax6 has been shown to be involved in the development of these light-sensitive structures, suggesting that Pax6 is a conserved protein that is crucially involved in eye development regardless of adult structure. Appropriately, the fruit fly version of the Pax6 gene has been named *eyeless*, because when the protein is nonfunctional due to mutation, the flies don't develop eyes at all. This protein is such a powerful initiator of eye development that when it is experimentally expressed in cells that would eventually develop into a wing or a leg, it causes the formation of an extra eye. And perhaps most amazingly, the structure of the Pax6 protein has been so conserved throughout evolution that when researchers experimentally force the *mouse* version of the protein to be expressed in a competent region of a developing fruit fly, extra eyes (the complex compound eyes of fruit flies) form where this mouse Pax6 is expressed.

Pax6 is crucial in initiating cell proliferation in the region of the presumptive eye, controlling retinal development, and interacting with a host of other proteins to link the eye structures into the central nervous system. But where did this essential protein come from? Pax6 is one of several closely related proteins, coded for by a group of extremely similar genes, all of which perform a wide variety of functions throughout the developing embryo. In those animals that immediately predate the evolution of eyes, such as the cubozoan jellyfish, scientists have found a single gene called PaxB that likely gave rise to the multiple Pax genes in subsequent animals. Scientists hypothesize that a gene duplication event occurred in this jellyfish that gave rise to what today we know as Pax6 and *as well as to another Pax gene*. These two Pax duplicates acquired different functions throughout the embryo, and Pax6 became crucial to the formation of the eye. Thus, although Pax6 initiates a wide variety of eye-development trajectories across the animal kingdom, the gene itself appears to have arisen at one point and to have ultimately retained its function, and thus made possible the evolution of the eye.

Thus, developmental biology supports the concept of the evolution of the adult eye as the result of an interacting genetic signaling module that evolved as an increasingly intricate unit, not a collection of independently-arrived-at parts. As the most basic signaling framework for eye development (the genetic cascades initiated by Pax6) seems to have been established with some of the earliest eyes, the subsequent modifications on this genetic system often involved recruiting unique cellular functions that had previously existed for other purposes in the developing embryo. For instance, many of the different types of crystallin proteins found in the lens of the eye serve completely different functions elsewhere in the body, such as in metabolism and protection from heat shock. However, as these proteins have unique light-directing qualities when they are packed close together, they seem to have been recruited to the developing eye at some point during evolution.[22]

The formation of the many interacting parts of the eye is thereby closely linked on a genetic level during development. Developmental biology has highlighted the idea that the so-called different parts of a developing organism are often linked by gene expression such that the formation of one part triggers the formation of the second part, which triggers the third, and so on. This process is by no means just linear—sometimes the second part will reinforce the formation of the first part or cause the first part to develop further. Regardless of the order, all the parts are interconnected in development. Thus, the vertebrate eye can form by reciprocal induction, wherein the parts are created by each other (and are not preformed entities that must somehow come together). Moreover, the eyes among the animal kingdom are not so many new themes but are variations on the theme of Pax6 designating the specification of the photoreceptors.

Contemporary evolutionary developmental biology studies the mechanisms by which small genetic changes can cause major anatomical changes (which, if selected, can cause evolutionary innovation). Scientists have found four ways by which Jacob's evolutionary "tinkering" occurs.[23] In the first three, the structural gene remains constant, but what changes are its regulatory regions—the enhancers and promoter—which flank the gene and tell it where, when, and how much product to transcribe. The first mechanism, *heterotopy*, involves a change in which cells express the gene. Thus, the webbed feet of ducks can be shown to have evolved from the separated feet of chicken-like birds by the production of the Gremlin protein in the interdigital webbing of the embryonic hindlimb. Heterotopy also explains how the turtle gets its carapace, and how the snakes lost their limbs. The second mechanism, *heterochrony*, involves changing the timing of gene expression between generations. It can explain the dolphin's elongated flippers and the young marsupial's strong forelimbs, among many other examples. The third mechanism, *heterometry*, involves increasing or decreasing the activity of a gene. Heterometry explains the evolution of the beak morphologies in Galápagos finches and also how certain human populations have greater immune protection against worm parasites. The fourth mechanism, *heterotypy*, involves an actual change in the structural gene. The evolution of insects from other arthropods (and why they have only six feet) involves heterotypy.

As Jacob had predicted, these are genes that are involved in constructing the embryo. Evolution is caused by inherited changes of development between generations. Thus developmental genetics can postulate mechanisms of large evolutionary changes. Moreover, these hypotheses can be tested on extant populations.[24] Heterometry of the BMP4 gene is associated with the changes of beak morphology in the Galápagos finches; adding activated BMP4 to chicks' beaks will cause them to broaden. The blocking of BMP signaling by the Gremlin protein is associated with the retention of the duck's hindlimb webbing; by adding Gremlin proteins to embryonic chick feet, one gets webbing like that of a duck.

This ability to postulate the genetic events behind structural evolutionary changes makes evolutionary developmental biology a vital front for ID proponents. Most creationists have long conceded the battle over microevolution (evolution within the species) to the biologists.[25] So what if a mosquito develops resistance to DDT? It's still a mosquito. If the AIDS or influenza virus evolves, they're still the AIDS and influenza viruses, respectively. These microevolutionary questions don't concern the Intelligent Design advocates. The battleground is now macroevolution: How can evolution explain how we get limbs and fish have fins, or how we have hair and not feathers or scales on these limbs? Such questions are the ones at stake, and this is what evolutionary developmental biology claims to be solving. Therefore, it is important for the Intelligent Design proponents to uncouple genes from development, to try to prove that genes do not control development. This need, I suspect, is why Wells is pushing the bizarre interpretation of his experiment, claiming that frog genes do not control frog head formation. I suspect that this motive is also behind Wells's *Icons of Evolution* as well as the article by Wells and Paul Nelson that attacks homology without mentioning gene sequences.[26] I think that the divorcing of genes from development is also critical for Intelligent Design not only because genes and gene sequences are producing our best evidence of homology (as in the chromosome 2 sequence of humans compared with the chimp genome), but also because the genetic sequencing prevents our definitions of homology from becoming subjective or tautological. Because of gene sequences, we can discuss descent with modification in ways that our predecessors a century ago could not.

CODA: WHY BIOLOGY?

My colleague, the evolutionary biologist Colin Purrington, has asked the question: "Why biology?" Why aren't Intelligent Design advocates protesting physics classes that claim the earth revolves around the sun ("the heliocentric theory is just a theory") or math classes claiming that the value of pi goes against what one finds in 1 Kings 7:23? Why aren't geologists fighting against creationist demands that the flood story be taught alongside plate tectonics ("one must keep an open mind, and plate tectonics was once thought wrong, too")? Why should such Christians get so upset about the postulated mechanisms for biodiversity?

I believe the answer has less to do with evolution being perceived as the enemy of Biblical literalism than it has to do with evolution being perceived as the enemy of Divine Providence. If there is a single element that characterizes biology-versus-religion debates across the whole spectrum of social concerns, it is that evolutionary biology has no special place for the human species. Evolutionary biology is adamant that Homo sapiens is an animal like any other, subject to the same natural forces as other animals, and also subject to extinction like any other animal. When evolutionary biology books (and even introductory biology books) show illustrations and cladograms depicting humans in relation to the other animals, humans are often placed on the same level as bears, flies, and any other living organism. The axis is time, not complexity, number of cells, or cognitive abilities. There is no top-of-the-tree position for humanity. Indeed, evolutionary biologists claim that the animals formed by evolution are contingent, and that "if the tape were to be played again," humans might or might not come into existence.[27] But contemporary Christianity claims that humans are special to God, that

God incarnated himself as a human, and that God has a plan of salvation for each human and for the entire human species.[28]

Thus, evolution is seen to call into question the grand design of Divine Providence. Even if the Deity does exist, evolutionary biology finds no evidence that God has any particular cares for the success and well-being of the human species. This issue was specifically addressed by the International Theology Commission of the Catholic Church (then under the leadership of Cardinal Ratzinger, the present Pope Benedict). While its 2004 Curia document "Communion and Stewardship" claimed that "even the outcome of a truly contingent natural process can nonetheless fall within God's providential plan for creation," the logic of this conclusion can be difficult to follow. But the core is that "neo-Darwinians who adduce random genetic variation and natural selection as evidence that the process of evolution is absolutely unguided are straying beyond what can be demonstrated by science." In other words, the absence of data (concerning a plan) cannot be read as evidence for the absence of a plan.

This message will not soothe those who demand that science conform to their theological expectations. Indeed, the chicanery of the type perpetrated by Intelligent Design proponents can only work if there is a public desperate for their message. And their message is "you are part of God's plan." The desire of Americans that there be a Divine plan for humanity can be seen in the debates concerning not only evolution, but also in the debates surrounding abortion, global warming, and the emergence of outbreaks of new viral diseases. It is not Biblical literalism that is at stake (for then, the physics and geology classes would be picketed), but human worth.

Let me give an example from a somewhat unexpected source: the outbreak narratives of infectious disease. Heather Schell and Priscilla Wald have each documented that the narratives of emerging infectious disease are structured to prevent our facing the distinct possibility of human extinction. Because we don't want to face the possibility of our own extinction through the simple indifference of nature, we add human agency to the infection narratives. In Wald's words, "We make it our fault, we make it something we can do something about."[29] The viruses are coming after us because of our stupidity, hubris, or avarice. However, the evolutionary view, enunciated by Joshua Lederberg, does not see human agency as so important. Microbes are microbes; they fight for survival, too. "We live in evolutionary competition with microbes—bacteria and viruses. There is no guarantee that we will be the survivors."[30] In the popular book *The Hot Zone*, Richard Preston declares, "The Marburg virus . . . did not know what humans are; or perhaps you could say that it knew only too well what humans are: it knew that humans are meat."[31] We might not win. There is no plan for human success or survival. In two hundred years, the human species may be extinct, all our wonderful civilizations will have ended, and no one will remember us. This is a horrific thought. It is what scientists must confront and use their knowledge to prevent. It is what some evangelical Christians feel they must deny. And this denial forms the basis of Intelligent Design.

Thus, the battle of evolutionary biology versus Intelligent Design is not a biological issue. It is a sociological confrontation, and it is not surprising that some of the best analyses of the struggle have come from sociologists. Dorothy Nelkin, in particular, has written eloquently and very evenhandedly on the creation controversy.[32] Seeing scientific creation as a symptom of social change, her analyses are still excellent a quarter of a century later. Intelligent Design, like its predecessor scientific creationism, is not science. It does not respect evidence, it celebrates ignorance, and its mathematics use nonscientific assumptions. However, it is useful to those who believe that God has a plan for each of us, and that God cares for the human species. It provides a counterweight to the scientific appropriation and dismissal of questions concerning the ultimate meaning of life. As such it is important. This was what Nelkin was saying, and this is the message that I repeat today. Nelkin noted the scientific arrogance of her time; and it hasn't gone down any since then. Criticism of some of science's claims to authority over religious attitudes needs to be made. But it must be made honestly. Intelligent Design is no substitute for honest criticism, and it should not be doing the work of those social critics who would like to see science playing a less dominant role in our culture.[33]

There is still no reason why we should permit religious doctrine to be taught in our science classes as an alternative for the evolutionary explanations of biodiversity. As I have tried to show, Intelligent Design is more in the tradition of American hokum than it is in any tradition of Western philosophy or theology. Personally, I think teaching the controversy is a good way to expose students to what science is. I am hoping that teachers will be able to give their students documents such as this book and the *Kitzmiller* decision and discuss what biology is and what it isn't. However, few high school science teachers (or for that matter university professors) feel themselves equipped to teach philosophy of science or sociology. And unless a teacher wants to introduce some sociology into his or her biology course, there is no reason to "teach the controversy" as part of biology.

The Classroom Controversy

A History of the Dispute over Teaching Evolution

EDWARD J. LARSON

When speaking at colleges and universities around the country, I frequently ask students what they learned about organic origins in high school. On the one hand, most of them tell me that evolution was touched on only lightly if at all. On the other hand, even fewer report receiving any creationist instruction. Mine is an unscientific survey, to be sure, but it accords with what others find. Origins has become the third rail of high school biology.

The American controversy over creation and evolution is primarily fought over what is taught in our public high school biology classes. Almost no one disputes teaching the theory of evolution in public colleges and universities or using public funding to support evolutionary research in agriculture or medicine. It is the minds of American high school students that are at stake.

Although the controversy has ebbed and flowed over the years, it goes back at least to the 1920s, when America's teenagers first began attending high school in great numbers. There they encountered the theory of evolution in their biology classes, provoking objections from some parents, taxpayers, and religious leaders. In most cases, these objections sprang from religious concerns, and the reason is obvious. Religion addresses great questions of life. Why are we here? Where did we come from? Where are we going? To the extent that science addresses these questions, it is treading on holy ground. More than any other concept in science, the theory of organic evolution—particularly as applied to humans—raises these issues.

Tension has long existed between religious and scientific ways of understanding the origins of life, individual species, and humanity. When asking about origins, philosophers and scientists from the time of the ancient Greeks have recognized two alternatives. Either the various species were specially created in some way or they evolved from preexisting species. The former view tends to stress the importance of a divine Creator while the latter view pushes back or eliminates a Creator. Both views have religious implications.

With the rise of Christianity, special creation dominated Western thought. For centuries, mainstream science (or "natural history" as it was called) supported this view of origins. Species appear fixed, early natural historians observed, and breed true to form. They do not evolve. Even more critically, as European natural historians came to appreciate the delicate balance in nature and within each living thing, many of them saw it as evidence of a Creator's existence and of that Creator's loving character and purposes. Particularly in the Protestant realms of Britain and Northern Europe, where science gained in cultural authority during the 1600s and 1700s, natural history became the handmaiden of natural theology.

Beginning in the 1700s, Enlightenment skeptics in France revived evolutionary thinking. Some deists and atheists argued that species must have evolved from preexisting species, but they failed to propose a plausible means of evolutionary development. Due in part to the tenets of natural history, creationism retained the upper hand in Western thought until the mid-1800s. Charles Darwin's theory of evolution by natural selection transformed the terms of this debate by supplying a logical explanation for how species evolve. Every offspring naturally differs from its parents and siblings, Darwin argued. A purely naturalistic struggle for existence selects the fittest of these offspring to survive and propagate their beneficial variations. In this manner, new species gradually evolved from preexisting ones, each delicately fitted for their environment without the intervening hand of God. Most biologists quickly accepted evolution as the source of new species, but many others did not.

Three overlapping levels of religious opposition to Darwinism emerged, and remain apparent today. In a narrow sense, any theory of evolution conflicts with a literal reading of the Genesis account, which declares that God specially created each kind of living thing during six days of creation. Accepting the Genesis account as literally true inclines believers to accept special creationism in biology and reject modern geologic theories that the earth is millions of years old. In a broader sense, the natural theology of Darwin's theory of evolution by natural selection troubles many theists. What sort of God would create living things through random chance mutations and a selfish struggle for existence? God could still use evolutionary processes operating over eons of time to develop the current diversity of life, these critics acknowledge, but not purely naturalistic ones. In the broadest sense, the total exclusion of God from any role in the origin of life strikes religious believers as presumptuous, if not preposterous.

None of these concerns constitute scientific objections to the modern neo-Darwinian synthesis that dominates Western biological thought, and their proponents do not offer any compelling scientific alternatives to that theory. Virtually all biologists accept the view that current species evolved over time from preexisting species, with many of them seeing little or no role for God in the process. In contrast, most Americans believe that God had a hand in the origin of species, with many of them opting for special creation over theistic evolution as God's means of creation. In a democracy with compulsory school laws and public schools, this division plays out every day in public school biology classes around the country. Parents, students, teachers, and taxpayers informed by the dominant scientific view of origins insist that the biology curriculum stress evolution. Many of those committed to a Biblical view want some place for creation in the science classroom.

Critics of teaching the standard scientific view of evolution in public schools typically propose one or more of three basic remedies. They argue that the schools should either 1) remove the theory of evolution from the classroom altogether, 2) balance it with some form of creationist instruction, or 3) teach it in some fashion as "just a theory." Actually these three strategies, although always present to some extent, also neatly play out chronologically so as to create three discernable phases of antievolutionism.

First came the phase characterized mainly by efforts to remove evolution from the high school biology classroom altogether, highlighted by the 1925 trial of John Scopes. Importantly, these efforts coincided with and arose out of the so-called fundamentalist crisis within American Protestantism, when many mainline Protestant denominations—the Presbyterians, Methodists, American Baptists, and others—split between the so-called modernists, who adapted their traditional beliefs to current scientific thinking, and a new breed of fundamentalists who clung to Biblical literalism in the face of new ideas.

No idea divided modernists from fundamentalists more than the Darwinian theory of human evolution—and the rift was aggravated by the seeming rise in agnosticism within the cultural and scientific elite. From the first, the fundamentalist-modernist controversy raged over the interpretation of Genesis in the pulpit. By the 1920s, both sides had carried that theological dispute into the classroom. Neither side wanted the other's view taught as fact in public school biology courses. In 1922, fundamentalists across the land began lobbying for laws against teaching the Darwinian theory of human evolution in public school, leading to the passage of the first such statute in Tennessee during the spring of 1925. Lesser restrictions had already appeared in other places and, like the current debate over Intelligent Design (ID), the overall issue had gained national attention.

From the outset, the "anti-evolution crusade" was seen as evidence of new and profound cleavage between traditional values and modernity. The crusade did not necessarily cause the cleavage, but it did expose it. In the mid–nineteenth century, Americans tended to share common values (or at least those Americans of Protestant European roots that set the tone). There were atheists, agnostics, and deists at the time, but they were marginal, and theological disputes among Christians rarely disrupted denominational harmony. Even the academy was a conventionally religious place—that is, until the rise of positivism, Biblical higher criticism, and Darwinism late in the nineteenth century. By the early twentieth century, surveys and studies began detecting a widening gap between the God-fearing American majority and the disbelieving cultural elite. It was not that the elite wanted to reject God or Biblical revelation, commentator Walter Lippman explained at the time, it was rather that the modern, naturalistic ways of thinking make God and revelation unbelievable. Indeed, it was the scientific method as applied to all facets of life more than any particular scientific theory that lay at the heart of modernity—but Darwinism was critical in applying that method to the key issues of biological origins and human morality.

The Tennessee antievolution statute thus struck a chord that resonated widely. The nationwide attention garnered by its passage soon focused on Dayton when a local science teacher named John Scopes accepted the invitation of the ACLU to challenge it in court. The media promptly proclaimed it "the trial of the century" as this young teacher (backed by the nation's scientific, educational, and cultural establishment) stood against the forces of fundamentalist religious lawmaking. For many Americans at the time and ever after, the Scopes trial represented the inevitable conflict between new-fangled scientific thought and old-fashioned supernatural belief. By this time, the conflict had long roots.

Ever since Charles Darwin published his theory of evolution in 1859, some conservative Christians have objected to the atheistic implications of its naturalistic explanation for the origins of species, particularly of humans. Further, some traditional scientists—most notably the great Harvard zoologist Louis Agassiz—promptly challenged the very notion of biological evolution by arguing that highly complex individual organs (such as the eye) and ecologically dependent species (such as bees and flowers) could not have evolved through the sort of minute, random steps envisioned by Darwinism. Although the scientific community largely converted to the new theory due to its ability to explain other natural phenomena that appear utterly senseless under a theory of design or creation (such as the fossil record and the geographic distribution of similar species), religious opposition remained, with these religious opponents often invoking the earlier scientific arguments against evolution. These religious objections naturally intensified with the spread of fundamentalism during the early twentieth century.

The legendary American politician and orator William Jennings Bryan, a political progressive with decidedly orthodox religious beliefs, added his voice to this chorus during the Twenties, as he came to see Darwinian survival-of-the-fittest thinking (known as social Darwinism when applied to human society) behind World War I militarism and postwar materialism. Of course Bryan also held religious objections to Darwinism and he invoked Agassiz's scientific arguments against it as well—but his fervor on this issue arose from his social concerns. Equate humans with other animals as the product of purely natural processes, Bryan reasoned, and they will act like apes. With his Progressive political instinct of seeking legislative solutions to social problems, Bryan campaigned for restrictions against teaching the Darwinian theory of human evolution in public schools, leading directly to the passage of Tennessee's antievolution statute in 1925. He then volunteered to assist the prosecution when his law was challenged in Dayton—foreseeing the pending show trial as a platform from which to promote his cause.

The prospect of Bryan using the trial to defend Biblical religion and attack Darwinism drew in Clarence Darrow. By the Twenties, Darrow unquestionably stood out as the most famous criminal defense attorney in America. His trials were sensational, with Darrow pioneering techniques of jury selection, cross-examination, and the closing argument to defend his typically notorious clients in bitterly hostile courts. Outside the courtroom, Darrow used his celebrity status and oratorical skills to challenge traditional morality and religion. At the time, most Americans clung to Biblical notions of right and wrong—with Darrow's defendants usually quite wrong. Darrow, however, with his modern mind, saw nothing as really wrong (or right)—everything was culturally or biologically determined. For him, dogmatic beliefs springing from revealed religion were usually the real culprit, by imposing narrow standards, dividing Americans into sects, and making people judgmental. Just as Bryan hailed God as love and Christ as the Prince of Peace, Darrow damned religion as hateful and Christianity as the cause of war. Indeed, Darrow saw rational science—particularly the theory of organic evolution—as offering a more humane perspective than any irrational religion. This left no grounds for compromise between him and Bryan. Both men were affable enough, and actively cooperated on some issues, but their worldviews were at war.

The prospect of Bryan and Darrow litigating the issues of revealed religion versus naturalistic science and academic freedom versus popular control over public education turned the trial into a media sensation then and the stuff of legend thereafter. It attracted hundreds of reporters to Dayton and generated front-page stories around the world. Broadcast live over the radio, in time it became the subject of Broadway plays, Hollywood movies, and Nashville songs. Clearly *Scopes* remains the best-known misdemeanor trial in American history. Despite Darrow's eloquent pleas for academic freedom and his humiliating cross-examination of Bryan, Scopes ultimately lost the case and Tennessee's antievolution statute was upheld. In large part, this resulted from the fact that the U.S. Supreme Court had not yet extended the constitutional bar against government establishment of religion to public schools.

When it was all over, most neutral observers viewed the trial as a draw so far as public opinion was concerned. America's adversarial legal system tends to drive parties apart rather than to reconcile them. That certainly happened in this case. Despite Bryan's stumbling on the witness stand (which his supporters attributed to his notorious interrogator's wiles), both sides effectively communicated their message from Dayton—maybe not well enough to win converts, but at least sufficiently to energize those already predisposed toward their viewpoint. If, as the defense claimed, more Americans became alert to the danger of placing limits on teaching evolution, others (particularly evangelical Christians) became even more concerned about the spiritual and social implications of Darwinian instruction.

Consequently, the pace of antievolution activism actually picked up after the trial (especially in the South), but it encountered popular resistance everywhere. Arkansas and Mississippi, for example, soon followed Tennessee in outlawing the teaching of human evolution, but when one Rhode Island legislator introduced such a proposal in 1927, his bemused colleagues referred it to the Committee on Fish and Game, where it died without a hearing or a vote. A forty-year standoff resulted in which a hodgepodge of state and local limits on teaching evolution, coupled with heightened parental concern elsewhere, led most high school biology textbooks and many individual teachers largely to ignore the subject of organic origins voluntarily. As a result, after the state supreme court reversed Scopes's conviction on a technicality, courts did not have another chance to review antievolution laws until the 1960s. By then, the legal landscape had changed dramatically.

The change began in 1947, when the U.S. Supreme Court grafted the First Amendment bar against religious establishment to the liberties protected from state action by the Fourteenth Amendment. Suddenly the Establishment Clause took on new life. Whereas Congress had rarely made laws respecting an establishment of religion prior to 1947 (so that there was little case law on the point), states and their public schools had been doing so right along. This led to a torrent of Establishment Clause litigation. Soon *Scopes*-like legal battles over the place of religion in public education began erupting in communities across the land, giving the old trial new relevance everywhere.

The first of these cases did not address restrictions on teaching evolution, but they surely implicated them. In successive decisions beginning in 1948, the Supreme Court struck down classroom religious instruction, school-sponsored prayers, mandatory Bible reading and, in 1968, antievolution laws. These old laws simply banned the teaching of human evolution—they did not authorize teaching other theories. Indeed, in his day, Bryan never called for including any form of creationist instruction in the science classroom, because no scientific alternative to evolution then existed. Even he believed that the Biblical days of creation symbolized vast ages of geologic time, and said as much on the witness stand in Dayton. With the publication of *The Genesis Flood* in 1961, however, Virginia Tech engineering professor Henry Morris gave believers scientific-sounding arguments supporting the Biblical account of a six-day creation within the past ten thousand years. This book spawned a movement within American fundamentalism, with Morris as its Moses leading the faithful into a promised land where science proved religion. The appearance of so-called creation science or scientific creationism (its proponents use both terms) launched the second phase of the antievolution politics: the phase associated with seeking balanced treatment for creation science.

Creation science spread within the church through the missionary work of Morris's Institute for Creation Research. The emergence of the religious right carried it into politics during the 1970s. Within two decades after the publication of *Genesis Flood*, three states and dozens of local school districts had mandated "balanced treatment" for young-earth creationism along with evolution in public school science courses. It took another decade before the Supreme Court unraveled those mandates as unconstitutional in *Edwards v. Aguillard*, which voided Louisiana's creationism law. Scientific creationism was nothing but religion dressed up as science, the High Court decreed in 1987, and therefore was barred by the Establishment Clause from public school classrooms along with other forms of religious instruction. By this time, however, conservative Christians were entrenched in local and state politics from California to Maine, and deeply concerned about science education.

THE REAPPEARANCE OF INTELLIGENT DESIGN

Although every phase of antievolution activism involved a popular movement composed of many actors, one figure stood out in each. If the first phase was associated with Bryan and the second with Morris, then the third phase can be tied to University of California law professor Phillip Johnson. Johnson was no young-earth creationist when he entered this fray, but he was (and is) an evangelical Christian with an uncompromising faith in God. His target became the philosophical belief and methodological practice within science that material entities subject to physical laws account for everything in nature. Whether called "naturalism" or "materialism," such a philosophy or method excludes God from science laboratories and classrooms. "The important thing is not whether God created all at once [as scientific creationism holds] or in stages [as theistic evolution maintains]," Johnson asserted. "Anyone who thinks that the biological world is a product of a pre-existing intelligence . . . is a creationist in the most important sense of the word. By this broad definition at least eighty percent of Americans, including me, are creationists."[1] If public schools cannot teach scientific creationism because it promotes the tenets of a particular religion, Johnson's argument runs, then at least evidence of intelligent design in nature or scientific dissent from Darwinism should be permissible.

Johnson took his concerns to the church. In a series of books published by Christian presses over the past fifteen years, Johnson has argued that science education should not automatically exclude supernatural explanations for natural phenomena. He calls on educators to question the sufficiency of Darwinism to explain life and urges them to teach the controversy over evolutionary naturalism in the classroom. After all, Johnson argues, evolution is just a theory, and not a very good one at that.

Johnson's books have sold several hundred thousand copies, and it is no wonder that his kind of arguments now show up whenever objections are raised against teaching evolution in public schools. They were apparent in the U.S. Senate in 2001 when Pennsylvania Senator Rick Santorum, a prominent evangelical, introduced legislation encouraging teachers "to make distinctions between philosophical materialism and authentic science and to include unanswered questions and unsolved problems in their presentations of the origins of life and living things."[2]

This language, penned by Johnson, passed the Senate as an amendment to the No Child Left Behind education bill and eventually became part of the conference report for that legislation. Similar proposals surfaced as stand-alone bills in over a dozen state legislatures during the past five years. None has passed yet. State and local school boards offer an alternative avenue of attack, with several of them imposing restrictions on teaching evolution or opening the door to creationist instruction.

Another popular authority on Intelligent Design is Lehigh University biochemistry professor Michael Behe, a devout Catholic who wrote his own best-selling book challenging Darwinist explanations for complex organic processes. Harkening back to a pre-Darwinian era in natural history, Behe revived traditional arguments for design based on evidence of nature's irreducible complexity.

Behe and Johnson do not argue for the young earth of creation science, but they do propound that intelligent design (rather than random chance) is apparent in nature. This, they argue, divorced from Biblical creationism, should be a fit subject for public school education. With this argument, they have expanded the tent of people willing to challenge the alleged Darwinist hegemony in the science classroom beyond those persuaded by Morris's argument for a young earth. Indeed, since most Americans believe that God played at least some part in organic origins, acknowledging the possibility of intelligent design strikes many people as both fair and reasonable. A 2005 public opinion survey suggested that two out of three Americans favor teaching some form of creationism alongside evolution in the public schools.

Some observers have labeled ID as the new creationism, but in its basic approach it is much older than creation science. Indeed, design theorists follow a venerable intellectual tradition associated with the likes of the British natural theologian William Paley, the French naturalist Georges Cuvier, and even the American politician William Jennings Bryan—all of whom saw an orderly creation testifying to its Creator and none of whom relied strictly on the Bible to reach that conclusion. Like their intellectual forebears, proponents of Intelligent Design represent various religious perspectives and reach out beyond fundamentalists to evangelical Protestants and conservative Catholics. Together with scientific creationists, they reject methodological naturalism in science and object to teaching Darwinism as fact. Although ID has yet to gain the mass following of creation science, its partisans now played a pivotal role in evolution-teaching controversies.

Yet the bedrock for antievolutionism in the United States remains the Biblical literalism of the Protestant fundamentalist church, where there is typically greater concern about the earth's age (to which the Bible speaks) than about such intellectual abstractions as scientific naturalism. In *The Genesis Flood*, for example, Henry Morris stressed the theological significance of utter fidelity to the literal truth of the entire Biblical narrative. Thus, when Genesis says that God created the universe in six days, he maintained, it must mean six, twenty-four-hour days; when it says that God created humans and all animals on the sixth day, then dinosaurs must have lived alongside early man; and when it gives a genealogy of Noah's descendants, believers can use it to date the flood at between five to seven thousand years ago. The influence of this sort of Biblical literalism, which typically sees the meaning of scriptural passages as being as readily understandable to believers as cookbook recipes, is no longer limited to old-line fundamentalists, but touches many Pentecostals, evangelicals, conservative Catholics, Mormons, and (so far as the Genesis account is concerned) Orthodox Jews. By most accounts, over half of the American people count themselves among these groups.

Despite judicial rulings against the incorporation of scientific creationism into the public school biology curriculum, opinion surveys suggest that about two out of every five Americans support the basic tenets of Biblical creationism as espoused by Morris and his Institute for Creation Research. If not propagated in the public schools, then creationism must spread by other means—and conservative Christian religious organizations have the necessary structures in place. Fifty years after its initial publication, *The Genesis Flood* (now in its forty-second printing) continues to sell well in Christian bookstores, but is now only one in a shelf-full of such books. Christian radio and television blankets the nation with creationist broadcasts and cablecasts, such as Ken Ham's "Answers in Genesis," which is now heard on over five hundred radio stations in forty-nine states. Although still relatively low in absolute terms, the number of students receiving their primary and secondary education at home or in Christian academies has steadily risen over the past quarter century, with many such students learning their biology from creationist textbooks. At the postsecondary level, Bible institutes and Christian colleges continue to grow in number and size, with at least some of them offering degrees in biology and science education in a creation-friendly environment.

All this creationist activity is nearly invisible outside the churches and religious communities where it occurs. Indeed, the secular media largely lost interest in scientific creationism once *Aguillard* squelched efforts to introduce it into public education. After that 1987 ruling, however, Biblical creationists turned inward to entrench their views within America's vibrant conservative Christian subculture. There they flourish, unchallenged and virtually inaccessible by evolutionists.

The spread of creation science and Intelligent Design has provoked some evolutionists. To be sure, most evolutionary biologists simply ignore religion. But some of them—ardent in their evolutionism and evangelical regarding its social implications—have taken a Darrowesque dislike to Christianity. The British sociobiologist and popular science writer Richard Dawkins leads this pack.

In *The Blind Watchmaker*, published to great acclaim in the midst of legal wrangling over Louisiana's creationism law, Dawkins takes aim at what he calls "redneck" creationists and "their disturbingly successful fight to subvert American education and textbook publishing." Focusing on the philosophical heart of creationism, rather than simple Biblical literalism, Dawkins challenges the very notion of purposeful design in nature, which he calls "the most influential of the arguments for the existence of God."[3]

In a legendary articulation of this argument in 1802, William Paley compared living things to mechanical watches. Just as the intricate workings of a watch betrayed its maker's purposes, Paley reasoned, so do the even more intricate complexity of individual organs (such as the eye) and of organisms prove the existence of a purposeful Creator. Not so, Dawkins counters. "Natural selection, the blind, unconscious, automatic process which Darwin described, and which we now know is the explanation for existence and apparently purposeful form of all life, has no purpose . . . It is the blind watchmaker." By banishing the argument for design, Dawkins proclaims, "Darwin made it possible to be an intellectually fulfilled atheist."[4]

Renowned Harvard naturalist and science writer E. O. Wilson makes assertions similar to those of Dawkins. "The inexorable growth of [biology] continues to widen, not to close the tectonic gap between science and faith-based religion," Wilson wrote in 2005. "The toxic mix of religion and tribalism has become so dangerous as to justify taking seriously the alternative view, that humanism based on science is the effective antidote, the light and the way at last placed before us."[5]

Organized science has sought to distance itself from the likes of Dawkins and Wilson by affirming the comparability of modern evolutionary naturalism and a personal belief in God. The National Academy of Sciences (NAS), a self-selecting body of the nation's premiere scientists, had asserted as much in a glossy brochure distributed to school teachers during the 1980s in reaction to the creation science movement. In 1998, the NAS mass-produced a new booklet reasserting that, while science is committed to methodological naturalism, it does not conflict with religion. They simply represent separate ways of knowing. "Science," the booklet states, "is limited to explaining the natural world through natural causes. Science can say nothing about the supernatural. Whether God exists or not is a question about which science is neutral."[6]

The eight-thousand-member National Association of Biology Teachers (NABT) took a similar tack as the NAS. In a position statement initially adopted during the 1980s in opposition to creation science and always controversial among theists, the Association had defined evolution as "an unsupervised, impersonal, unpredictable and natural process of temporal descent with gradual modification," which is a fair depiction of the modern Darwinian theory. In 1997, responding to heightened sensitivity to the atheistic implications of Darwinism, the Association's executive committee voted to delete the words "unsupervised" and "impersonal" from the statement. The group's executive director explained, "To say that evolution is unsupervised is to make a theological statement," and that exceeds the bounds of science.[7]

The NABT move surprised many. A *New York Times* article described it as "a startling about face." To Dawkins, it represented "a cowardly flabbiness of the intellect." Johnson dismissed it as rank hypocrisy. If they agree on nothing else, Dawkins and Johnson agree that Darwinism and Christianity are at odds—and, with their writings and talks, they help to stir popular passions over biology education much as once Darrow and Bryan did. We see its fruit even now in pending lawsuits and current legislation.[8]

TWENTY-FIRST-CENTURY LEGAL BATTLES

The third phase of antievolution activism in the United States has produced a new generation of legal restrictions. In Kansas during 1999, for example, creationists on the state school board succeeded temporarily in deleting the Big Bang and what they called "macroevolution" from the list of topics mandated for coverage in public school science classrooms. Six years later, they took the further step of adding an ID-friendly definition of science to their educational standards. In 2004, the suburban Cobb County, Georgia, school board decreed that biology textbooks should carry a disclaimer stating that evolution was just a theory. One year later, the rural Dover, Pennsylvania, school board mandated not only an oral disclaimer akin to Cobb County's written one but also recommended Intelligent Design as an alternative explanation of biological origins. In cases that made front-page news across the country and overseas, federal district courts promptly struck down the Cobb County and Dover restrictions. Both decisions are instructive.

In the course of revising its science curriculum generally, the Cobb County school board directed that biology textbooks carry a sticker stating, "Evolution is a theory, not a fact, regarding the origin of living things. This material should be approached with an open mind, studied carefully, and critically considered." Similar disclaimers have appeared in Alabama textbooks for years without sparking lawsuits and are under consideration elsewhere but, perhaps because the diverse nature of the county's population and its visible location as a bedroom community for Atlanta, the disclaimer immediately encountered stiff opposition in Cobb County. The Georgia ACLU promptly filed suit on behalf of some local students and their parents.

In his 2005 judicial opinion, Judge Clarence Cooper tackled

antievolutionists' "only a theory" argument. Of course evolution is only a theory, but it's not a hunch or a guess, he noted. "The Sticker targets only evolution to be approached with an open mind, carefully studied, and critically considered without explaining why it is the only theory being so isolated as such," he wrote. In light of the historic opposition to the theory of evolution by certain religious groups, Judge Cooper concluded that "an informed, reasonable observer would perceive the school board to be aligning itself with proponents of religious theories of origins." As such, the sticker constituted an impermissible endorsement of religion under prevailing constitutional standards, the judge ruled.[9]

Although Judge Cooper did not expand on the point, he identified the group benefited by the sticker as "Christian fundamentalists and creationists," not theists generally. Many people see the controversy this way, which helps to explain its depth. Millions of American Christians and other religious believers accept the theory of evolution. For some theologically liberal Christians, evolution is central to their religious worldview. Even many theologically conservative Protestants and Catholics accept organic evolution as God's means of creation. They see no conflict between it and a high view of scripture. Theistic theories of evolution have a long and distinguished pedigree within evangelical Christian theology. By cautioning students against all theories of evolution, some saw the Cobb County school board lining up on one side of a dispute among religious believers and in doing so unconstitutionally entangled church and state. Judge Cooper agreed—and held this as a second legal basis for striking the stickers.

The Dover case, like the Cobb County one, involved school guidelines built on the ID argument that students should be told that evolution is a controversial and unproven theory. "The theory is not a fact," the Dover disclaimer stated. "Gaps in the theory exist for which there is no evidence." Following similar legal reasoning as Judge Cooper, in 2005, Pennsylvania federal district court Judge John E. Jones III concluded that this mandated statement constituted an unconstitutional endorsement of a religious viewpoint.

Unlike the Cobb County sticker, however, the statement read to Dover students added, "Intelligent Design is an explanation of the origin of life that differs from Darwin's view. The reference book, *Of Pandas and People*, is available for students who might be interested in gaining an understanding of what Intelligent Design actually involves." This text, Judge Jones found, contained creationist religious material, including the affirmation that basic kinds of living things (such as birds and fish) were separately created. As such, its use in a public school science class violated the constitutional bar against religious instruction much like teaching creation science would.

The decision went further, though. During a six-week trial, Judge Jones heard extensive testimony on Intelligent Design to determine whether it could be presented as an alternative explanation of origins in a public school science class. Here his decision broke new ground. "After a searching review of the record and applicable case law," Jones ruled, "we find that while ID arguments may be true, a proposition on which the Court takes no position, ID is not science." He gave three reasons. First, unlike science, ID invokes supernatural explanations. Second, it rests on the flawed argument that evidence against the current theory of evolution supports the design alternative. Third, scientists have largely refuted the negative attacks on evolution leveled by ID theorists.[10]

In reaching his conclusion that ID is not science, Judge Jones noted that it has not been accepted by the scientific community, generated peer-review science articles, or been subjected to testing and research by scientists. Significantly, Michael Behe conceded all these points under cross-examination during the trial. Indeed, to assert that ID nevertheless belonged in a biology classroom, Behe offered an alternative definition for science that he claimed was commonly used by scientists even though not formally accepted by scientific organizations. "A scientific theory," he posited, "is a proposed explanation which focuses or points to physical, observable data and logical inferences." On cross-examination, however, Behe conceded that his ID-friendly definition of science would also admit astrology into the realm of science even though he could not think of any scientists who believed in it. This admission alone may have sealed the judge's decision, but evidence that some Dover school board members acted with a clear religious purpose in adopting their science statement and then tried to cover their tracks also turned this judge, a no-nonsense conservative appointed by President George W. Bush, against the school policy. "The breathtaking inanity of the Board's decision is evident when considered against the factual backdrop which has now been fully revealed through this trial," he concluded.[11]

THE ROAD FORWARD

Despite their holdings, the Cobb County and Dover decisions are unlikely to resolve the American controversy over teaching evolution in American public schools any more than the Scopes trial did in 1925 or the *Aguillard* ruling did in 1987. At most, these 2005 rulings, like their predecessors, may help to shape the legal and political landscape for the next phase of the dispute. Three factors tend to limit the effect of these two rulings.

First, federal district courts issued both rulings. District courts stand at the bottom rung of the federal judiciary hierarchy. Their rulings apply only to their geographical districts, which in these cases are Northern Georgia and Middle Pennsylvania. Beyond their districts, judicial rulings are instructive only. Given their clear exposition of applicable constitutional law, these rulings may discourage school boards in other areas from imposing written or oral disclaimers of the types mandated by the Cobb County and Dover school boards. School boards and individual teachers can express their concerns about the theory of evolution in other ways, however, and may be more likely to do so in the wake of these rulings.

Second, the losing party in a district court case can appeal the ruling, which the Cobb County school district once did. Federal circuit court rulings supplant federal district court rulings and have wider direct impact and instructive influence. The losing party in a circuit court case can request review by the U.S. Supreme Court. In the first two phases of antievolution lawmaking, it took rulings by the Supreme Court to dispose of the specific matters at issue: in 1968 by striking down Arkansas's law against teaching evolution and in 1987 by voiding Louisiana's law requiring balanced treatment for creation science. Those decisions changed the legal landscape and channeled antievolution activism in new directions. Ultimately, only a Supreme Court decision may resolve the place of Intelligent Design in American public schools.

Third, even the Supreme Court cannot finally settle the matter. Regardless of what any court decides, teaching the theory of evolution in public schools will continue to create controversy so long as a significant percentage of Americans hold religious objections to it. Earlier Supreme Court decisions against antievolution and balanced-treatment laws simply altered the terms of the debate somewhat and provided a reason for more conservative Christians to seek parochial education for their children. They did not change what people believed.

The United States remains a deeply religious nation. Public opinion surveys invariably find that over nine in ten Americans believe in God—just as they have found since surveys began polling on such matters in the 1950s—with most of them asserting that religion is "very important" in their lives. It troubles many that science does not affirm their faith and outrages some when biology textbooks seem to deny it. Lawsuits and legal decisions cannot resolve fundamental cultural or religious disputes. They can draw clear constitutional lines, however, and those lines can influence behavior and beliefs over time. With education and understanding, change happens. Perhaps better science education and deeper understanding of the popular appeal and scientific limits of the Intelligent Design concept can help both sides to appreciate the vital place of both scientific knowledge and religious faith in the evolving American experience.

Untangling Debates about Science and Religion

JANE MAIENSCHEIN

In September 2005, I entered the Federal Building and U.S. Courthouse in Harrisburg, Pennsylvania, and joined a line of citizens passing through security and heading to the hearing rooms upstairs. Nearly everyone was there for the case of *Kitzmiller v. Dover Area School District*, being heard by Judge John E. Jones III. I was there at the request of the Federal Judicial Center's Education Division to lead an all-day seminar on science and social issues surrounding embryo research, including cloning and stem cells. One of the judges in my seminar commented that conflicts about science and religion seem never to go away, but that the same old debates just emerge in new forms. He wasn't sure that anybody ever really learns anything along the way, though I am a bit more hopeful than he.

At lunch, we joined Judge Jones, who felt it was already very clear what should count as good science and also that for constitutional reasons science and not religion should be taught in schools. We all agreed that the public is often given the impression that what is at stake is a simple battle of science versus religion—as if that were just one straightforward debate and as if it were just a matter of determining which of two clearly defined sides will win. Was the *Dover* trial (or are the apparently similar debates concerning whether to allow human embryonic stem cell research in the United States) simply a straightforward controversy over whether science or religion will win?

The answer, of course, is yes. But not really. Or not only. The Intelligent Design controversy, like the stem cell controversy, is a tangle of debates over several distinct questions operating on very different levels. Some of these can be resolved with increased understanding and communication, through various versions of compatibilism or translation between science and religion. Some of the issues are superficial. Some come from deep and abiding differences in underlying assumptions and are irresolvable. By laying out the tangle of issues more clearly and separating the various threads, we can promote tolerance and enlightenment rather than intolerance and misrepresentation.

There are two different kinds of unificationist extremists: those advocating religion as an ultimate arbiter and unifier that provides morals and metaphysics, and those advocating all and only science all the time and denying any role for other values or views in modern society. Both hold to their convenient coherent worldviews and their tightly woven tangle of views. Each denies authority to others with competing views, and they allow no room for compromise or compatibilism. These are the extremes, and most people lie in between.

On the one side, ID proponents, like their "creation science" predecessors, create confusion about what is really meant by science and by religion and then take excellent advantage of the resulting confusion. They demand that we, as a society, teach "the controversy"—as if it were clear what that is. The media then take up the call for understanding the controversy about science and religion in the form of evolution and creationism, and demand "balance" without understanding across which variables there must be balance. Public discussion then swirls about "the" debate and "the" controversy. The same thing has happened with those demanding protection for embryos that they define as persons and over which definition they claim to have moral authority, and they portray themselves as in opposition to those who want to do research. It is instructive to look at these two cases.

At the same time, as Michael Ruse has energetically pointed out, including quite publicly and personally in an email exchange with Dennett posted on the blog Uncommon Descent, ardent anti-religion evolutionists like Richard Dawkins and Daniel Dennett do not help the situation.[1] In such books as Dennett's *Breaking the Spell* and Dawkins's *Blind Watchmaker*, they paint their pictures in terms as stark as those of the creationists, suggesting that evolutionary science is good and science is right on all matters, and that there is neither need nor room for religion. We also find Nobel laureates such as geneticist Paul Berg recently giving a distinguished lecture at Arizona State University's Law School, and stumping energetically for stem cell science. He claimed that all scientific research is good and that there is even a constitutional right to free inquiry through research. Both those opposing the particular science in question and those advocating all and only science as good call for laying out and playing out "the" controversy. Extremists on both sides seem to want either religion or science clearly to win. The evolution-creationism debate, the stem cell debate, the . . . fill-in-the-blank science-versus-religion/morality debate: each is taken as a straightforward us-versus-them set of polarities.

There is danger in not untangling the web of beliefs. If we allow the false impression that there is a simple controversy at work here, the group with the most unified, simplistic, and unchanging set of premises has the easiest position to argue. Those holding an apparently coherent and nicely integrated view resist untangling the intertwined threads that make up their "worldview," and the apparently integrated coherence and the certainty and ardor with which its advocates hold the view are seductive to many. Even for those of us who choose to embrace no religion, or those of us who feel that preimplantation embryos are just cells "in a dish," it is important to realize the range of views and the reasonableness of some of them but not others—and to develop a set of socially shared criteria for which views are reasonable and which are not. Above all, it is important to recognize and embrace the complexity of the natural and the social worlds. "It is," as Darwin noted on the last page of his 1859 *Origin*, "interesting to contemplate a tangled bank, clothed with many plants of many kinds, with birds singing on the bushes, with various insects flitting about, and with worms crawling through the damp earth, and to reflect that these elaborately constructed forms, so different from each other, and dependent upon each other in so complex a manner, have all been produced by laws acting around us."[2] That bank is tangled with a natural world of organisms and also a social context of metaphysical, epistemological, and moral assumptions.

Untangling the bank brings understanding of the fundamental natural laws and social practices that govern its existence. As thinkers from Isaac Newton to the philosophes to current scientists have agreed, science such as evolution provides our best available approach and methods for understanding and explaining the natural bank. Indeed, as Darwin continued in his last paragraph, "There is grandeur in this view of life, with its several powers, having been originally breathed into a few forms or into one; and that, whilst this planet has gone circling on according to the fixed law of gravity, from so simple a beginning endless forms most beautiful and most wonderful have been, and are being evolved."

Yet this is not to argue that there can be nothing beyond science and the material, nor that through science we have any way of knowing what might or might not be beyond the natural material world. In the later editions of the *Origin*, Darwin himself allowed—at least logically—for both the natural laws of science and for a creator. In later editions, he revised his final clause to: "having been originally breathed by the Creator into a few forms or into one." There can be room for science and a creator, as long as the roles are carefully and clearly untangled and defined. There is room for a "god of the gaps," as the role has come to be called.

Let me be perfectly clear what is not at issue. From the perspective of the biological sciences, there is absolutely no question that a form of evolution of species by natural evolution has occurred, including evidence that the human species has arisen through a process of natural selection and other natural forces. Furthermore, we would be foolish to behave or believe otherwise because there are consequences in not accepting this understanding brought by an overwhelming mass of scientific evidence. There is too much at stake in human evolution and what we can expect for our future not to accept this scientific evidence that evolution has occurred and explains how the organic world got to be this way. Many, many converging lines of evidence support this conclusion. We do not have the whole story yet, of course, nor should we expect to. But the coherent picture that emerges and that is reinforced by new discoveries is completely unambiguous scientifically. Scientifically, there is no controversy. A large number of churches recognize this fact, as seen on February 12, 2006, which became "Evolution Sunday." This is not the place to rehearse the case for evolution. There is no scientific controversy, and as Kenneth Chang showed in the *New York Times*, even the feeble attempts to claim that "scientists" question whether evolution has occurred center on short lists of engineers and nonbiologists who are said to have questions.[3] There is no doubt, there is no evidence against evolution, and there is no controversy about the science of evolution.

SCIENCE VERSUS RELIGION: WHY THE CASE OF HUMAN EMBRYONIC STEM CELLS IS RELEVANT

Arguments about human embryonic stem cell research and whether we should allow it, fund it publicly, regulate it, or prohibit it altogether play out in similar ways, though some of what is at issue is different. Let us be very clear here as well. "The" debates are not about science versus morality, which is (falsely) assumed by some to come only from religion. This is not about choosing between the wishes of wild-eyed scientists to do research no matter what versus the wise and moral superiority of those who would protect the most innocent of human lives. Yet the public presentation often makes it seem that the issues are the same: science versus morality or religion. Again, we need to untangle issues.

In the case of embryos, what biology shows is that there is a point in time for each individual organism, under normal circumstances, when an egg cell is fertilized by a sperm cell and that zygote begins to split into more and more cells. Biological research makes it clear that the earliest divisions divide material and do not produce growth or any significant gene expression. Cells just divide into smaller parts. This continues up to the blastocyst stage, at which point most of the cells divide quickly into more and more small cells that are called the embryonic stem cells and that make up an inner cell mass. This is surrounded by a single layer of cells that will eventually make up the placenta. At this stage, the preimplantation embryo is called a blastocyst.

This stage in human development is a ball of cells bouncing around in the mother's uterus and just beginning to move toward implantation in the uterine wall, or else the blastocysts are in the "dish" in a fertility clinic where some will be placed into a potential mother for implantation, others will be frozen for later implantation, while still others will be discarded. At this point in the history of biological research, human blastocysts cannot develop further and cannot begin differentiation without having become implanted in the mother. This is the biological knowledge, clearly explained by leading developmental biology textbooks such as Scott Gilbert's and by educational explanations about stem cells on the NIH website;[4] the science is as well founded and as solidly grounded and unquestioned as evolution.

Further, as far as we know, every one of these stem cells in the blastocyst stage of the embryo before implantation is capable of becoming any one—but not all—of the different types of cells that make up the body. Hence each is considered pluripotent, with plural potencies, but it is not totipotent since it cannot become a whole organism by itself. Which type of cell any one pluripotent cell will become in normal conditions depends on signaling among all the cells in the individual organism, and that depends on each cell's environment. Researchers have discovered that by controlling the environment of each cell, through different cell culture media, they can cause each undifferentiated cell to multiply and generate a cell line and also with different media to become differentiated as different types of cells.

There is no disagreement about the major facts. Of course, researchers are making new discoveries and adding tremendously to our knowledge, as they are in understanding the details of how evolution works. But there is no scientific controversy here. Biological researchers agree that we can and should learn more about how development and differentiation occur. Nobody seriously argues that we should not seek to gain further knowledge about embryos. Understanding is good in science.

The discovery of these pluripotent cells is also exciting for po tential therapeutic applications for two reasons: first because researchers might actually be able to culture specific desired types of cells for medical use, and second because study of these cells and what makes them differentiate in different ways informs our understanding of how we might produce particular kinds of cells with the right engineering. The potential is clear and well established, though we do not yet know what it is actually possible to do with human embryonic stem cells.

Controversies begin to arise, however, when we ask which research should be done and how. Should we study human development by taking human blastocysts and harvesting stem cells in order to study them? Right now, the only way we know how to study human embryonic stem cells is to open up the blastocyst and remove the cells. This stops any further development of the blastocyst. Harvesting embryonic stem cells therefore necessarily "kills" the embryo. Science—as science—entails no view about whether this is a morally bad or good thing. Scientifically, for purposes of understanding more about nature through science, the act can be "good" (in the sense of justified) if harvesting stem cells produces reliable new knowledge. In the strictest sense of science, then, there is—there can be—no controversy over stem cell research. Controversy comes from our metaphysical and moral interpretations, which lie outside of science. For some, embryos at the blastocyst stage are persons or potentially persons, and therefore deserve protection and at least the "respect" not to have research done on them. For others, at this early stage these are just cells in the dish. Biology tells us very clearly what the cells can do and what they can do by virtue of being together, as an organism. Biology cannot tell us whether these cells should be considered persons or what moral, legal, or religious interpretations we should have about them. Society as a whole has to do that, and the attempts to do so have been much disputed in many overlapping and cross-cutting debates outlined in numerous books, articles, and websites.

That is to say, we develop a socially accepted metaphysics. As a society, we accept that there is a natural world, made up of natural objects that consist of matter and motion. Nobody denies that, not really. As Boswell noted in his *Life of Johnson*, when Bishop Berkeley confronted Samuel Johnson with arguments that matter might not really exist, Johnson reportedly kicked the large stone nearby and exclaimed, "I refute it thus." Matter exists and it is kicked by external agents or it moves and changes (or develops or evolves) under certain conditions. What is less easily demonstrated is the metaphysical claim that there is more to the world than that matter and its motion. Perhaps there is also a set of supernatural values and beings. Perhaps a blastocyst is really a person in some sense that deserves moral and legal respect or protection. Science cannot answer such questions; they require nonscientific methods such as introspection, intuition, or faith. Therefore, we come here to epistemological debates. Scientists acting in their roles as scientists rely on empirical observation and rational explanation as the way to know about the world. Science may draw on, but as science does not rely on, appeal to introspection, intuition, or faith. Religion relies precisely on these methods.

We now have two sets of debates: metaphysical debates about the nature of what exists in the world, and epistemological debates about how we should go about knowing about it. These debates have become more obvious and contested in different ways with human embryo research. Scientists have their views about what is right and good, but they accept the need for social and political resolution of the moral issues. Some of those moral imperatives, and even some religious injunctions call for carrying out scientific research. For example, traditional Jewish values place highest priority on saving lives even if that means using stem cells from early embryonic stages that are not considered persons in Jewish law. Meanwhile, extreme embryo protectionists accept that there may be scientific needs but feel that their own moral considerations should trump when there is conflict.

Both metaphysical and epistemological differences are also at issue in debates about evolution. "The controversy" has been set up such that the extremes of antireligion scientists and antievolution creationists have staked their positions in strong terms and in opposite corners. They have allowed public discussion to develop as if this were a matter of science versus religion. Yet we are back to the need to tease apart the different threads of what is really a tangle of debates.

UNTANGLING ISSUES

For those who see the world in terms of integrated holistic worldviews, different threads of commitment and belief are entangled. Probably inevitably, we each hold some set of entangled views, and doing so is convenient. It keeps us from having to think about every single episode that comes along and decide our view on that particular case. Yet some individuals and groups find it useful to entangle even more threads and hold them tightly together. We each make decisions about which threads to accept as given, and the question then is how many we hold true in this way and what we do when one is questioned.

Science requires questioning, discovery, and skepticism, leading to interpretations and reinterpretations in the light of new knowledge. Many religions allow questioning and discovery as well, of course. Yet some, including fundamentalist antinaturalist religious views, do not. I would like to believe that most people would embrace scientific questioning and discovery about the natural world and would appeal to other compatible views about moral and metaphysical views beyond what science can provide only where necessary to fill the gaps, if only they were given that choice. We must work to give them that choice, beginning with honest worldview untangling. There are many different ways to untangle the threads, of course, but for our purposes here, we can focus on five sets of issues that cut across metaphysical and epistemological issues.

Evolution versus Creation (as Theories Explaining How the Organic World Has Come to Be as It Is)

Both science and religion ask the question, "How has the organic world come to be as it is?" One Intelligent Design debate, then, is at root epistemological: Should we address that question with the scientific methods of empiricism and interpretation, or do we appeal to faith and introspection? Historically all versions of "creation" stories have invoked a creator outside the material world and rely on other than scientific authority for such claims. Thus, we have questions about how far science can take us and what we need to fill the gaps that remain.

Some religious extremists prefer to see a conflict between science and religion, and they assert that we can know about the world only through religious revelations. Similarly, some scientists prefer to see conflict when they go beyond science to insist that only science can give us any sort of knowledge. Scientists acting scientifically cannot establish that there was no creator, since that claim lies outside the bounds of scientific testability. We can say that there is no—and cannot, given the foundations of scientific method, be any—scientific evidence of any supernatural creator. But that, of course, will hardly be compelling for the religiously inclined who find their evidence elsewhere.

Those who wish to do so can appeal to other values and methods, including metaphysical views from religion, to assert the existence of a creator. Others will prefer to invoke values such as parsimony or metaphysical materialism to argue against the existence of any supernatural being or forces that we cannot experience through material senses. These differences are often laid out as religion versus atheism (or antitheism), and sociologically the debates often take that form. Yet logically, what we have is a difference of theism and nontheism. That is, from the scientific, naturalist methods and knowledge, we cannot know that there is no deity. Whereas atheists actively deny the existence of a god, nontheists hold that the question of whether or not there is a god is irrelevant and unknowable. We can only know that the category makes no sense within science and that it requires other values and views to invoke such a non-natural thing.

Evolutionism (or Scientism) versus Creationism (as a Worldview)

Let us pursue further these distinctions about what can be known within science and what requires additional claims external to science. Scientists understand that only science can give reliable, justified *scientific* knowledge and evolutionism is a special case where evolution provides the knowledge, in particular about how species arise and what makes the organic world as it is. Extreme proponents of evolutionism, including notably Dennett and Dawkins, profess that they know that evolution and science are all there is. As Ruse has discussed clearly, such views are unwarranted and evolutionism taken too far becomes "belief" in the sense of unsupported doctrine. To be clear: I am not claiming that evolutionary science is belief in this sense; it is not. Rather, evolutionism as a philosophical position goes beyond science. To reiterate: science itself gives us no way of knowing that there is nothing beyond science and the natural world.

It has been in the interest of some extreme evolutionists to attack all creationists for their lack of scientific reasoning and to see them as denying any science, which is not fair. There are many people who believe in some sort of limited first origins type of creation (indeed, I suspect nearly all of them except the maniacal) who perfectly well accept that there is a natural world and even that science will give us the best knowledge about most of it. But they deny that science can give us everything we need to understand how any species arose (for those who deny evolution altogether), how humans arose (for those who envision a special creation for man), or how life or the universe began in the first place (for those who allow a naturalistic role for evolution but not for first origins).

Conversely, it has been in the interest of creationists to attack evolutionists for rejection of a creator and to imply that this leads down a slippery slope. The strongest forms of this completely un-justified attack claim that because evolutionists deny that the human species was specially created, therefore they have no moral values including no valuing of human life. This is absurd, of course, since most evolutionists perfectly well accept that there are values and so-cial interactions that go beyond evolution and even that human life has value. Rather, the value and the process of evaluation lie outside science and its methods.

Evolutionary biologists claim neither that evolution provides all answers to everything, nor that science can answer everything. Nor is the acceptance of values outside of science *per se* a problem for the doing of science. We expect a diversity of ideas in a pluralistic soci-ety. Science gives us the best way of knowing about the natural and organic world, but other values and ways of knowing may also have a role—and this is important—only insofar as they do not contradict the claims of the sciences about the natural world.

With respect to our views of embryos, most citizens fall some-where between the extreme that says that the fertilized egg cell is a person deserving of full legal protections and that therefore no research should be allowed on cells derived from it, even if they would be thrown away otherwise, and the extreme that says that re-searchers should be allowed to do anything they want at any time. Most citizens are also experienced enough to realize that extreme hopeful hype (stem cell research will lead to solutions for all medical problems you can imagine) and fear-mongering (stem cell research will turn us into uncaring Nazis) are both unwarranted extreme positions.

There is, in other words, a great range of possible ways to find compatibility of different epistemological and metaphysical views and values. Science and evolution, creation and values: all can reside together as long as we are fair-minded, tolerant, and recognize the boundaries and limits. This is not the place for further detailed discussion of demarcation criteria between science and religion, but rather to note that comfortable compatibilism can occur in diverse ways.

Process and Change versus Fixity and Given

Another debate intersects the others and concerns the extent to which we see properties of change and process rather than fixity and stability in the world. With evolution, it is obvious that those accepting evolutionary explanations for how the natural world came to be this way accept that there has been change. Creationists accept a range of types of change, but extreme conservative creationists want much to be given and fixed. They claim that a creator must have created, that the world goes on without much change, and that they know what is true and right even if others—indeed even if most others—disagree. This shows the extent to which some are uncomfortable with the idea of any change. The desire to control change feeds back into desire for a solid and predictable interpretation of the world, which does not work well with the continual inquiry and discovery of the scientific approach.

The differences play out in interesting ways in the embryonic stem cell debates. Here, some scientists themselves have appeared to embrace the stability perspective, and this has perhaps reinforced social interpretations of what an embryo is. Geneticists, in promoting their program by (over)emphasizing the importance of genes in causing effects, have created a misimpression. The public has a strong sense that genes cause development, fairly directly, so that "genes are us." This leads to a sort of preformationist thinking, as I explain in more detail in *Whose View of Life?*, with the impression that once an individual organism has its full complement of genes lined up along chromosomes, it is effectively determined and just grows and plays out the program already encoded genetically. Unfortunately, this geneticism also feeds the sense that the organism is fixed and that it is, in fact, already effectively the person it might become later. Such thinking is unfortunate in that it unintentionally reinforces a religious and social interpretation that lies outside science and holds that the individual's life begins at conception (typically meaning fertilization).

This is true in only the most limited sense. There are good reasons that a wide range of traditional views have seen life as beginning only with "quickening," typically taken as occurring at forty days. In fact, as we know now, genes are useless unless and until they are expressed during development. The first cell division process begins after fertilization, but gene expression, growth, differentiation, and other features of living organisms come only later. And we know that details of differentiation and morphogenesis are highly dependent on the context and the environment. Indeed, embryonic stem cell research has attracted such attention precisely because the differentiation process depends so much on context, the particular culture medium, and environmental stimuli, and because it allows such plasticity and responsiveness. It is therefore unfortunate that we are left with an excitement about process and change, but a background of mushy assumptions about preformation and fixity.

Secularism/Rationalism versus Religion/Spiritualism

As mentioned above, at least part of what is at issue is a debate about epistemology. What are the legitimate ways by which we come to know something? Do we achieve knowledge through reason, logic, and science, or through faith, introspection, and intuition? Once again, of course, these are not extreme polarities with no positions between. Many people, and again perhaps the vast majority, hold to some version of rationalism and naturalism with an emphasis on secularism in most aspects of their lives. Traffic directions, cooking, and other domains function by natural and social laws that are separate from religion. Airplanes fly, and we understand how they fly through science and engineering, and not through prayer, no matter how many passengers may engage in prayer while flying. Yes, for those who choose to do so, they may consistently accept scientific epistemology and yet also embrace some aspects of religion, even accepting that some types of knowledge may be grasped through faith—as long as faith does not deny the role of reason and science is accepted as the best approach for understanding the natural world. But no, it is not acceptable, given what we know about social norms, to deny that any reason exists and that everything is solely spiritual. We have bodies that do work at least in large part like machines, and nearly everybody in the developed world understands and takes care of those bodies based on scientifically driven material medical principles.

Stephen Jay Gould called science and religion "nonoverlapping magisteria" and they are that to some extent. Science and religion need not overlap. Yet, as Ruse and a number of historians of science have pointed out persuasively, they may. They may compete for authority, control, and power, but need not even if there are overlaps.[5]

Our social and legal norms help decide where the boundaries lie. Within the law, the U.S. Constitution makes one thing very clear. The First Amendment Establishment Clause has been interpreted as prohibiting public institutions from establishing religion in general or any one religion in particular. ("Congress shall make no law respecting an establishment of religion.") This has been taken as requiring that public education must remain secular and may not promote religion, and that directly affects what may be taught in schools.

What to Teach versus What to Require Being Learned

In public education, we have two different issues that go beyond basic views about epistemology and metaphysics and morals to the legal: the nonestablishment of religion, and also the impact of a shift from an emphasis on what teachers will teach to an emphasis on tests, focusing on what students should be required to learn. From the beginnings of public education in what became the United States at the Boston Latin School around 1645, public education has been taken to be a local matter. States hold authority to direct, and school districts to oversee and implement, curricular and instructional decisions. Most of these decisions have focused on textbook selection and on what to teach or not teach. It has always been easy to decide to teach reading, writing, arithmetic, science, along with areas such as history and social studies. Most issues have been about how much to teach and whether teachers are prepared to do the teaching and students to learn at the appropriate level. Two areas have often provoked considerable controversy, however: sex education and whether to teach evolution. Traditionally, these debates have played out locally, with periodic bursts of activity at the state and recently at the national level, ironically led by President George W. Bush, who on other issues has supported states' rights.

For example, Tennessee passed a state law in 1925, labeled the Butler Act, "prohibiting the teaching of the Evolution Theory in all the Universities, Normals and all other public schools of Tennessee, which are supported in whole or in part by the public school funds of the State, and to provide penalties for the violations thereof." Dayton teacher John T. Scopes challenged the law, which led to the highly publicized Scopes trial. Scopes lost, despite the rhetorical successes on his side, and the trial brought wide public awareness of debates about evolution and creation in this law that prohibited the teaching of evolution in Tennessee schools.

Only in 1968, when the Supreme Court agreed to hear *Epperson v. Arkansas* and ruled that laws prohibiting the teaching of evolution amount to an attempt to establish religion: only then was evolution taught in Tennessee's public school biology classes. As a student who graduated from high school in Oak Ridge, Tennessee, in 1968, I read Darwin's *Origin* in English class. Even in this highly educated, science-oriented high school, teachers were not allowed to adopt textbooks or teach evolution in biology classes until the courts forced them to do so, but our English teacher thought we should know about the ideas. Yet even after *Epperson* forced the states to allow the teaching of evolution, in 1973, Tennessee passed a law requiring that evolution be labeled "a theory" and that equal space be given in textbooks to "other theories," explicitly including the Genesis account of creation. Other state actions and court rulings have further defined the discussion about what is allowed.

These decisions have focused on what teachers are allowed to teach and what school districts are allowed to include. In the late 1990s, the discussion shifted. Yes, there are still discussions about what sex education or how much diversity study or which history, for example, will be allowed in classrooms, as well as whether and how to teach evolution. But instead of debates about what to allow, the discussion is now predominantly about what to require.

This changed with the growing national demand for "standards." This demand converged from a number of quite divergent directions. A frustration about the declining literacy and success rates among U.S. high school graduates raised the call for improved standards across the boards. In the sciences, leading scientific organizations such as the American Association for the Advancement of Science developed Project 2061 to guide science education, and the National Research Council developed its *National Science Education Standards.*

The impetus came from a general agreement that science education in this country was failing, and a coalition emerged among those concerned mainly about the low educational standards and those concerned about the declining American workforce. In addition, the U.S. Congress under Newt Gingrich's leadership of the House of Representatives both embraced science as a potential salvation and deplored the slide into poor quality. Republican leadership raised the call for standards—in science education, in education generally, in government agencies (with the Government Performance and Results Act of 1993). As the Government Accounting Office explains it, the Act "seeks to shift the focus of government decision-making and accountability away from a preoccupation with the activities that are undertaken—such as grants dispensed or inspections made—to a focus on the results of those activities, such as real gains in employability, safety, responsiveness, or program quality. Under the Act, agencies are to develop multiyear strategic plans, annual performance plans, and annual performance reports."[6]

This emphasis on plans and reports led educators to tests. How better to assess performance, state after state decided, than to develop tests? But what would be tested? Learning outcomes, they decided, based on standards. State after state began developing standards, outcomes, and tests. The No Child Left Behind Act signed into law in 2002 reinforced this approach. The Act emphasizes local freedom to develop standards and teaching plans according to local needs, but only if there are standards and tests and results that can be measured and compared. This is not the place to discuss the reasons for and against this approach, but rather to note that the decision has had effects. Now each teacher, each school, each school district, and each state has to make explicit decisions about what to teach and what to test.

This emphasis means, of course, that every state has to decide whether it will teach evolution and whether and how students will be tested on that teaching. The state of Arizona illustrates the kinds of local political debates that go on to determine what will be presented as good science in the schools and in the tests. In 1997, in the flush of enthusiasm about developing standards and forcing accountability, a committee was asked to develop a set of standards and present them to the Board of Education. They developed a draft, borrowing heavily as nearly all states did from the National Research Council's *Standards*. Alert school teachers discovered that the draft did not follow the NRC's standards completely, however, and had carefully omitted any mention of evolution.

The Board of Education appointed a review committee to assess the science standards and present a revised version. Each member of the Board appointed one member to the committee, with the result that the committee was divided as to whether to include evolution or not. I served on the committee at the request of Arizona State University's president, as did a colleague of mine, Steve Rissing, who was appointed by the Superintendent of Public Instruction and who has since been a leading advocate for teaching evolution in the state of Ohio.

Steve and I found deeply entrenched creationists on the committee. They realized that they could not block the teaching of evolution completely, since there was such strong support for it. So, they took one of the common approaches of insisting that we teach "the controversy." In 1997, the popular language was that we must "teach the evidence for and against" evolution. This approach had worked in some states, and it continues to be the main attempt to leverage some form of creationism into the curriculum and into the standards.

These creationists argued that no honest scientist can oppose teaching evidence. Surely science is about evidence, and about learning to weigh evidence for and against theories. Therefore, how can anyone object. Indeed, President Bush took this approach in his remarks in August 2005, commenting on the *Dover* case. He said of evolution and Intelligent Design that "both sides ought to be properly taught . . . so people can understand what the debate is about." And further, that "part of education is to expose people to different schools of thought . . . You're asking me whether or not people ought to be exposed to different ideas, and the answer is yes."[7]

Surely we can all agree that teaching about evidence is good. Evidence for and against theories. What we did in Arizona—and this approach has held through one major and several minor challenges—was to agree. We accepted the call to discuss evidence for and against—but for and against all theories, not just evolution. We took the "evidence for and against" clause out of its direct connection to "evolution," in other words, and made it a standard itself so that students have to learn about the nature of science and its use of evidence as applied to any ideas in science. This follows the NRC *National Science Education Standards* and the AAAS *Benchmarks for Science Literacy*, each of which emphasizes the nature and history of science.

Every student should learn about the methods and processes of doing science, including how to use evidence in assessing theories. Teachers will teach about evolution, natural selection, change over long periods of time, and the other core ideas of evolution. They will teach about what a scientific theory is—whether gravitational theory, molecular theory, or evolutionary theory. And they will learn about how scientists test theories and accumulate evidence to make them stronger, and about how accumulated evidence makes some theories so strong that we can take them as extremely well established and as the basis for predictions. We can treat them, in effect, as "fact." This is what we do with evolutionary theory. Now students know that evolution, like other theories of science, is not "just a theory," but that it has the tremendous power of a well-established scientific theory that is based on considerable accumulated evidence, is tested rigorously, and offers testable predictions. Evolutionary science has tremendous accumulations of evidence for and no scientific evidence against the science. The purported "evidence against" comes from outside science and does not stand up to scientific test. It is very useful to understand that such a "theory" holds the highest and most powerful status in science, alongside the theories of gravitation, a sun-centered universe, or genetic inheritance.

But, of course, this idea of "the evidence" is not what creationists want at all, even though in Arizona we managed to convince enough of them so that evolution and its central tenets did end up in the science standards. In fact, extreme evangelical creationists want to determine by themselves what will count as evidence against evolution. In Arizona, they wanted to dictate which textbook would count, and that is true in many states. A very few textbooks would be acceptable, and not coincidentally the authors of those textbooks have often actively campaigned to have their books adopted. This extremely significant profit motive cannot be ignored as motivator in the argument for "alternative" educational materials, though it is obviously only part of the story.

What is at heart for the true believers is just that—true belief. They believe that they are struggling for the hearts and souls of

American children. Science educators on the other hand, believe that science education should be a matter of struggling for the minds of those children. This is one point of conflict, and it takes us back to the sets of different controversies involved. For many creationists, the debate is about worldviews and values, and not really about science at all. They want to establish their values, their views, and their beliefs. And that brings us to the Establishment Clause and the *Dover* ruling.

DOVER

For Judge Jones, it is clear what schools should be allowed to teach in science classes: science and only science. Intelligent Design is not science and evolution is, he explained very clearly in his ruling in *Kitzmiller v. Dover Area School District*, in a ruling released December 20, 2005. The ruling seemed to many commentators like a lovely Christmas holiday gift to those advocating the fair and open teaching of evolution.

To review key features of the case: on October 18, 2004, the Dover school district's board had voted that "students will be made aware of gaps/problems in Darwin's theory and of other theories of evolution including, but not limited to, intelligent design. Note: Origin of Life is not taught." The school district then announced that teachers would be required to read to ninth-grade students the following statement:

The Pennsylvania Academic Standards require students to learn about Darwin's Theory of Evolution and eventually to take a standardized test of which evolution is a part.

Because Darwin's Theory is a theory, it continues to be tested as new evidence is discovered. The Theory is not a fact. Gaps in the Theory exist for which there is no evidence. A theory is defined as a well-tested explanation that unifies a broad range of observations.

Intelligent Design is an explanation of the origin of life that differs from Darwin's view. The reference book, *Of Pandas and*

People, is available for students who might be interested in gaining an understanding of what Intelligent Design actually involves.

> With respect to any theory, students are encouraged to keep an open mind. The school leaves the discussion of the Origins of Life to individual students and their families. As a Standards-driven district, class instruction focuses upon preparing students to achieve proficiency on Standards-based assessments.[8]

Tammy Kitzmiller and other parents filed suit challenging the constitutionality of the statement. They felt that this statement was a promotion of the philosophy of Intelligent Design in particular and that it amounted to an attempt to establish a religion in public schools. Judge Jones concluded that "for the reasons that follow, we hold that the ID Policy is unconstitutional pursuant to the Establishment Clause of the First Amendment of the United States Constitution and Art. I, § 3 of the Pennsylvania Constitution."[9]

Judge Jones's ruling very clearly untangles distinct issues and is helpful in promoting public understanding of what is involved in the multiple and tangled debates.

- First, there are claims about what should count as science: the ID proponents arguing that ID is science, and opponents arguing that it is not. Jones notes that this understandably depends on clear definitions of what science is and what authorities shall determine this.
- Therefore, the first question involves a second set of claims about what science is and who decides: with clearly articulated definitions and criteria laid out. Jones describes in detail the testimony of philosophers of science such as Robert Pennock in laying out the boundary criteria in clear, reliable, and verifiable ways. And it is clear that the scientific community of experts in a particular field should be the arbiters.
- Third are claims about whether ID is an attempt to establish religion in the schools: ID proponents arguing no, and

opponents arguing yes. This requires an understanding of the nature and realm of religion.

- Therefore, this third issue requires an evaluation of what counts as a religion and on what authority and evidence. Jones relied on the history of debates about evolution and creationism and what he saw as a compelling argument that ID is a continuation of previous antievolution creationist traditions.
- Finally, there are also discussions of what students should be allowed to learn and what they should be expected to learn, enforced through standards and tests.

This latter point was especially important in leading Jones to his ruling about this particular case. The second paragraph of the statement that the school district required to be read states that "Darwin's Theory is a theory . . . The Theory is not a fact." Judge Jones noted that in thus singling out evolution from the rest of science, it

informs students that evolution, unlike anything else that they are learning, is "just a theory," which plays on the "colloquial or popular understanding of the term ['theory'] and suggest[ing] to the informed, reasonable observer that evolution is only a highly questionable 'opinion' or a 'hunch.'"

This is a deliberate attempt to mislead, Jones argued, and the continuation of the statement pointing to gaps fails to note that there are gaps in other scientific theories as well. It is the singling out of evolution that ultimately caused Jones to rule that ID is not science and that it has no place in science classes in public schools.[10]

Jones rejected the ID proponents' claim that what they want is simply to teach "the controversy." There is no controversy, Jones concluded. Or rather there is no controversy within science. There is no controversy that belongs in public education. There is no controversy about science versus religion as "the" way of knowing about the natural world. He vigorously rejected the claim by ID proponents that their statement was not an attempt to teach ID but that they were only "making students aware of it." As Jones noted, "In fact, one consistency among Dover School Board members' testimony, which was marked by selective memories and outright lies under oath, as will be discussed in more detail below, is that they did not think they needed to be knowledgeable about ID because it was not being taught to the students. We disagree."[11]

Jones opted for a version of compatibilism, even if the ID advocates did not. He noted that "after a searching review of the record and applicable caselaw, we find that while ID arguments may be true, a proposition on which the Court takes no position, ID is not science." ID fails on three counts: it invokes supernatural causation, claims irreducible complexity, and offers attacks on evolution (like Michael Behe's) that have been rejected by the scientific community. ID is not a science. It may be true as religion, but that is not at issue.[12]

In his conclusion, Judge Jones makes the ID claims very clear and provides a strong argument for holding evolution and religion as compatible. "Both Defendants and many of the leading proponents of ID make a bedrock assumption which is utterly false. Their presupposition is that evolutionary theory is antithetical to a belief in the existence of a supreme being and to religion in general. Repeatedly in this trial, Plaintiffs' scientific experts testified that the theory of evolution represents good science, is overwhelmingly accepted by the scientific community, and that it in no way conflicts with, nor does it deny, the existence of a divine creator."[13]

Judge Jones's wise and well-grounded ruling is extremely important. It shows that both those who would seek to establish ID or other forms of religious creationism as science and those who would seek to establish that scientism leads to a rejection of a divine creator are unjustified in their beliefs. Evolution is not opposed to religion, just as embryo science is not opposed to morality. There is room for both, and there is room for social and political decisions about what form of compatibility we will embrace. What is clear is that the result cannot involve rejecting the study of evolution. Unlike the challenges with human embryonic stem cell research, where the very doing of the science raises special moral questions that scientists themselves recognize and that call for social and political resolutions, there are no such challenges with evolution. We need to study evolution, and not doing so has consequences.

WHY IT MATTERS: BUGS AND DRUGS

For many reasons, studying evolution is important, and indeed essential for a civilized society. I will focus just briefly on only two: study of human-host pathogen interactions, and biodiversity.

Take avian flu, or the H5N1 mutation of the virus. News reports track the progress of this virus around the world, and the Center for Disease Control is carefully tracking when it will arrive in the United States and whether and when it will jump from birds to humans. Many viruses have made this jump. And while only a few human cases of H5N1 infection have been reported yet, the virus is extremely contagious and it is very virulent in birds and humans, with a high death rate. Authorities around the world are on alert for the virus and its effects.

We would have no epidemiologically useful understanding of the virus without an understanding of evolution. Nor of HIV, nor any of the many other pathogens that affect animals and humans. Viruses and bacteria mutate. We understand mutation through genetics. But populations of viruses, and the particular strain of viruses that dominate, are the result of population change, natural selection, and evolution. Every year, the CDC and other health organizations around the world make their best guesses about the way evolution will work to develop the best possible influenza vaccines.

The bubonic plague pandemics of the fourteenth century, HIV epidemics, and other diseases that affect humans have evolved, and sometimes they evolve quickly. As a society, we use our science and technology to develop vaccines and antibiotics. Sometimes, however, the pathogens evolve faster than we are able to keep up. Some strains of tuberculosis pathogens have developed drug resistance, and some even multiple drug resistances. The only way to understand and have any hope of keeping ahead of such developments is through an understanding of population changes and evolution. A society that rejects understanding of evolution is one that cannot understand the behavior of the bugs that affect us, nor the drugs that will serve to treat our diseases. Nor can we understand bugs at a different level. To understand ants, termites, or bees—all social insects, with highly complex societies adapted to diverse environments—we need evolution. And only with understanding of evolution can we borrow lessons from these social communities.

A second important area requiring understanding of evolution is biodiversity. We seem to be losing numbers of species, as well as numbers of individuals within many species, at a drastically increasing rate. This matters for both instrumental and aesthetic reasons. We use many of the world's plants and animals as resources—for food and medicines. Furthermore, most human societies have valued animals and plants for aesthetic reasons. A green and leafy environment is more welcoming than a barren one. A land of milk and honey is more attractive than an arid barren land of winds and sand. Furthermore and most importantly, ecologists are demonstrating that we humans cannot survive without the support of a complex interactive ecosystem full of other life forms.

Therefore, we need understanding of evolution. We need the science, and there is also room to allow some versions of religion. Not narrow, evangelical, science-bashing religion, but open-minded, tolerant, and well-behaved religion. The sort of religion that I hope most fair-minded intelligent Americans who are inclined to embrace any form of religion will hold. Once we untangle the bank of issues, there is grandeur in this view.

Intelligent Design
A Symptom of Metaphysical Malaise

ROBERT MAXWELL YOUNG

Although I am not an expert on Intelligent Design or the history of creationism, my experiences in writing on Darwin and Darwinism and on metaphysical problems in the paradigm of explanation of modern science may be of some help in understanding some of the deeper issues behind this latest critique of Darwinism. Believers in Intelligent Design and some fundamentalists feel strongly that nature, living nature and human nature, cry out for an account that is more meaningful, richer, less desiccated, and more redolent of hope than the one on offer from the scientific reductionism advocated, sometimes in a bullying manner, by modern scientific materialists. I cannot support the idea of Intelligent Design. I wish to suggest, rather, that those to whom it appeals might look for hope and meaning in ways that are less simplistic and less in opposition to some of the grandest achievements of science.

INTRODUCTION AND STRATEGY

The theory of Intelligent Design usually has two premises. The first, though not always explicitly acknowledged and sometimes even denied by its proponents, is a privileged position for the Bible over all other repositories of knowledge. There are a number of manifestations of this view, the most stringent of which is Biblical fundamentalism or literalism (or inerrantism), whose advocates claim that every word of the Bible is the inspired word of God. It follows that if the Bible says that God created the heavens and the earth and all of life, including humankind, in six days, then it is literally so. Believers in Intelligent Design need not be strict Biblical literalists or even, at one extreme, specify what the Intelligence is. They can, for example, adopt various forms of Biblical realism, for example, believing that Biblical "days" were epochs or ages of considerable length (a position held by many in the nineteenth century, both before and after Darwin). Obviously, one can adhere strictly to "the Word of God" as it appears in the Bible in many ways, including, at the liberal extreme, taking account of the findings of Biblical scholars about the historical contingency of the Bible and other sacred or putatively sacred writings.

The second premise of Intelligent Design is that certain forms of life, or at least certain structures, cannot be scientifically accounted for by the mechanism of random mutation and natural selection, which is Darwin's basic explanation for the occurrence of evolutionary change—the entire history of life. This view is historically continuous with the argument from design or natural theology: something that strikes us as obviously contrived, for example, a watch, implies a contriver, that is, a watchmaker. It could not have come about except as a result of the action of an intelligent agent. Generalizing this argument, nature and life are so rich and complex that only a Divine Watchmaker, God, could have created the universe (see chapter 2). A third premise is implicit in those two—that God performs miracles as he did in the Old and New Testaments and is required to have done to bring about the astonishing and otherwise inexplicable changes which it is claimed that Darwinian evolution could not have brought about. Once again, not all advocates of Intelligent Design would be this explicit about the role of God in the history of nature, living nature and human nature.

Some believe that peace between religion and science can be

achieved by granting that God created the laws of nature and that the universe continues to obey them. I don't think this can be right according to most Christians. In that strand of Christianity which has been particularly receptive to the recent articulation of Intelligent Design, the idea of divine intervention has been especially prominent. I would say that most Christians believe that Christianity depends on suspending or superseding of the laws of nature in several claimed historical events (e.g., miracles are a precondition for sainthood in the Catholic Church). Ones that come to mind are the parting of the waters of the Red Sea by Moses, thus rescuing his people; the Incarnation; the Virgin Birth; the raising of Lazarus; the feeding of the multitudes (loaves and fishes multiplied, water turned into wine), the Resurrection of Christ from the dead. Don't most Christians believe that God intervenes in history whenever a sinner is saved? Otherwise, why believe in Christ's saving ministry and the divine purpose of His crucifixion?

I am clear about these things (or perhaps, it might be said, about certain versions of them), because I was brought up a fundamentalist in Texas, the fifth generation in our church and the son of a Presbyterian deacon and grandson of a missionary who worked in China at the time of the Boxer Rebellion. When I went East to university I took a course on religion (the first of many) in which the professor carefully spelled out the inconsistencies and contradictions in the accounts given in the four Gospels. I felt it right to go up after his lectures and point out his errors, interventions to which he reacted gently. More recently, I have read a more extensive scholarly account of the Bible by Robin Lane Fox, a distinguished Oxford classical historian, *The Unauthorized Version: Truth and Fiction in the Bible* (1991), in which he argues, *inter alia*, that Genesis presents two incompatible versions of Creation and that the story of the Nativity in Matthew and Luke is nonsensical. He treats the whole book as a human creation, full of problems for the believer.

Some years after my introduction to scholarly Biblical studies I addressed myself to the debate between science and religion surrounding Darwin's development of the theory of evolution by natu-

ral selection.[1] I have also devoted considerable energy to philosophical problems in the paradigm of explanation of modern science as
applied to the life sciences and to the understanding of human
nature (see the Further Reading section). In relating my findings in
these two realms to each other, I may be able to offer some insight
into the real philosophical problems that might be said to lie behind
Intelligent Design.

First, we shall sketch on a broad canvas the history of modern
reductionism and its problems. Then we shall see that Darwin had a
lot of sympathy with the central argument of Intelligent Design,
though he narrowly came down on the side of natural selection, albeit supplemented by rather a lot of other explanatory factors (not
including the direct action of God). Alfred Russel Wallace, the codiscoverer of the theory of evolution by natural selection, saw natural selection as adequate to explain almost all living nature, but, to
Darwin's dismay, he made an exception of the origin of man and,
in particular, the human brain, and employed the argument from
design in doing so. Intelligent Design has a long history, as Ruse
demonstrates, and it has taken other forms besides the current one.
I have no wish to support the antiscientific strand of this tradition,
only to note its venerable place in the history of the evolutionary
debate. Moreover, I know that many of the opponents of Intelligent
Design accuse its proponents, ironically, of bad faith and of covertly
pursuing a political agenda. I am not concerned with this aspect of
the debate. To the anticreationists I say, "Don't write off the whole
argument just because it may be made in a biased and simple-
minded way. There are deeper and more subtle issues at stake."

My larger purpose, however, is to draw attention to some features
of Darwin's argument, in particular the role of teleology and anthropomorphism at the heart of his theory, and then to connect these to
some fundamental issues in the paradigm of explanation of modern
science which have been put forward by some eminent philosophers, notably Alfred North Whitehead, Edwin Arthur Burtt, and
Peter F. Strawson. Doing so will draw attention to some deep short-

comings and evasions in the materialist reductionist paradigm of explanation of modern science, especially where the biological and human sciences are concerned. These shortcomings and evasions have left those who yearned for purpose and meaning in life and nature to complain that scientific explanation, at least in its current form, is just not enough. The consequent split between mechanism and purpose and a number of other splits subsidiary to it have left us with the problem of two cultures and an ongoing conflict between the arts and the sciences. The success of what Charles Gillespie called the advancing "edge of objectivity" that we owe to science has, unnecessarily in my view, worsened the split and led decent people to abjure the scientific worldview in certain respects. Meanwhile, certain of the advocates of science have been monumentally arrogant and tactless in trampling on the sensibilities of sincere people who have expressed their disquiet about the life sciences in a way that is, I grant, simplistic, but simplistic in a cause that has some philosophically defensible, even admirable, roots. The theological opponents of Darwinian evolution exemplify some legitimate criticisms of the reductionism of the modern scientific worldview. It is not that I agree with them, for my beliefs have come to lie (somewhat wistfully) somewhere between agnosticism and atheism, and I am a Darwinian. Rather, I think their opposition to the adequacy of scientific explanations of the earth, life, and human nature are symptoms of a legitimate malaise, one that merits some sympathy and which the scientific and philosophical communities need to address and, if possible, ameliorate.

THE PARADIGM AND ITS PRICE

The separation of fact and value that we associate with modern science lies at the bottom of the science-religion split, which was codified in the seventeenth century. The framework of explanation that prevailed in ancient and mediaeval times was the Aristotelian one in which causes or *aitia* (literally, the "comings to be" of things) always occurred in fours: the material, the efficient, the formal, and the final cause. If you did not come up with all four causes you did not have an explanation. Most of them are familiar to our modern scheme, because versions of them were carried over into the paradigm of explanation of modern science. The material cause told you out of what the effect came—the matter. Our modern concept of matter, including the periodic table of elements and of fundamental particles, corresponds to this. The material cause of an ordinary chair would be wood. The efficient cause is that which imparts energy to it and would include intrinsic ideas of energy not altogether unlike our own but also that which imparted change, in this case, the carpenter. The formal cause was hugely important in the writings of Plato and Aristotle, but we can only dwell on certain aspects—what type it was, where it sits in a classification. The chair could be said to partake of the form of "chair-ness," but the formal cause can embrace architects' plans, formal arrangements, structures, shapes, types, taxonomies. There were also forms for the good, the true, the beautiful, for humankind, for dishonorableness, for dirt, even for shit. As I say, there were and still are major debates about forms or types—where they come from and how we get them into our heads. People such as John Locke, Immanuel Kant, Jean Piaget, Noam Chomsky, and, in psychoanalysis, Wilfred Bion have pondered such things. The fourth and last explanatory factor was the purpose or use or aim and was called the final cause. The final cause of a chair is to provide somewhere to sit.

The first three of the four Aristotelian causes found their way into the explanatory paradigm of modern science, but the final cause was considered not objective and was split off and relegated to the minds of God and of people. It is not part of a scientific explanation, at least not a reductionist or materialist explanation. That's the official story, at least, but it kept sneaking back in, for example, in functional explanations in anatomy, physiology, and medicine, in evolutionary theory, in the functionalist tradition in the human sciences which was based on biological analogies, for example, social structures, social functions, and organic analogies. But make no mistake: strictly speaking, they had no place in the explanatory paradigm of materialist science, which allowed only matter, motion, and number to appear in explanations.

René Descartes, whose *Discourse on Method*, published in 1637 and often called the founding document of modern philosophy, was explicit about these issues concerning what counts as a scientific explanation. He divided the world into two sorts of things—extended substances and thinking substances. Extended substances had extension, figure, and motion and made up the world of matter, while thinking substances were defined negatively as that which does not pertain to matter, and their essence was will. We were left with a world of minds and bodies—since called Cartesian dualism.

The paradigm of explanation worked out by Descartes, Galileo, Isaac Newton, and others specified that no terms or concepts that are subjective, teleological (referring to purposes), or anthropomorphic (using categories belonging on the mental side of the mind-body split, especially ones referring to intentions) should appear in a scientific explanation. More or less enthusiastically, it was urged that people do experiments, but whatever the varying views on this issue, it was agreed that scientific conclusions should take the form of explaining all phenomena in terms of matter and motion. This injunction is summarized in the preface to Newton's *Mathematical Principles of Natural Philosophy* (1687): "All the difficulty of philosophy seems to consist in this—from the phenomena of motions to investigate the forces of nature, and then from these forces to demonstrate the other phenomena."[2]

This radical redefinition of reality was useful for certain scientific purposes, but it left a dreadful legacy of unsolved problems, for example, how minds and bodies interact. Many philosophers have lamented this split. One of my favorites is Alfred North Whitehead, coauthor with Bertrand Russell of *Principia Mathematica* (1910, 1912, 1913), one of the great mathematical works of all time and the foundation stone of modern symbolic logic. Late in his life Whitehead accepted an invitation to give the Lowell Lectures at Harvard. He stood back and reflected in *Science and the Modern World* (1925), in which he had this to say about the modern scientific worldview:

> The seventeenth century had finally produced a scheme of scientific thought framed by mathematicians, for the use of mathematicians . . . The enormous success of the scientific abstractions, yielding on the one hand matter with its simple location in space and time, on the other hand mind, perceiving, suffering, reasoning, but not interfering, has foisted onto philosophy the task of accepting them as the most concrete rendering of fact.
>
> Thereby, modern philosophy has been ruined. It has oscillated in a complex manner between three extremes. There are the dualists, who accept matter and mind as on equal basis, and the two varieties of monists, those who put mind inside matter, and those who put matter inside mind. But this juggling with abstractions can never overcome the inherent confusion introduced by the ascription of misplaced concreteness to the scientific scheme of the seventeenth century.[3]

Another philosopher who reflected on the consequences of the worldview of modern science was Edwin Arthur Burtt, who taught philosophy and theology at Cornell and wrote *The Metaphysical Foundations of Modern Physical Science* (1932). Reflecting on the consequences of this worldview for any attempt at understanding human nature, he said,

> It does seem like strange perversity in these Newtonian scientists to further their own conquests of external nature by loading on mind everything refractory to exact mathematical handling and thus rendering the latter still more difficult to study scientifically than it had been before. Did it never cross their minds that sooner or later people would appear who craved verifiable knowledge about mind in the same way they craved it about physical events, and who might reasonably curse their elder scientific brethren for buying easier success in their own enterprise by throwing

extra handicaps in the way of their successors in social science? Apparently not; mind was to them a convenient receptacle for the refuse, the chips and whittlings of science, rather than a possible object of scientific knowledge.[4]

Whitehead and Burtt are eloquent in their renditions of the consequences of Cartesian dualism for our ways of thinking about experience. Whitehead says,

> The occurrences of nature are in some way apprehended by minds, which are [somehow] associated with living bodies. Primarily, the mental apprehension is aroused by the occurrences in certain parts of the correlated body, the occurrences in the brain, for instance. But the mind in apprehending also experiences sensations which, properly speaking, are qualities of the mind alone. These sensations are projected by the mind so as to clothe the appropriate bodies in external nature. Thus the bodies are perceived as with qualities which in reality do not belong to them, qualities which in fact are purely the offspring of the mind. Thus nature gets credit which should in truth be reserved for ourselves: the rose for its scent; the nightingale for its song; and the sun for its radiance. The poets are entirely mistaken. They should address their lyrics to themselves, and should turn them into odes of self-congratulation on the excellency of the human mind. Nature is a dull affair, soundless, scentless, colourless; merely the hurrying of material, endlessly, meaninglessly.[5]

On the other hand, Whitehead grants that these abstractions have been enormously successful. The problem lies in accepting them as reality itself.

Burtt draws out the consequences of the paradigm in nearly identical terms:

> The world that people had thought themselves living in—a world rich with colour and sound, redolent with fragrance, filled with gladness, love and beauty, speaking everywhere of purposive harmony and creative ideals—was crowded now into minute cor-

ners in the brains of scattered organic beings. The really important world outside was a world hard, cold, colorless, silent, and dead; a world of quantity, a world of mathematically computable motions in mechanical regularity. The world of qualities as immediately perceived by man became just a curious and minor effect of that infinite machine beyond. In Newton the Cartesian metaphysics, ambiguously interpreted and stripped of its distinctive claim for serious philosophical consideration, finally overthrew Aristotelianism and became the predominant worldview of modern times.[6]

Limitations of space have precluded my spelling out the precise historical developments leading to the overthrow of Aristotelianism and the establishment of the materialist reductionist paradigm of explanation of modern science. This story is clearly spelled out in the books by Whitehead and Burtt that I have quoted.

DARWIN AS AN EXAMPLE OF THESE ISSUES

Darwin and Wallace's theory is an example of some features of the critique mounted by Whitehead and Burtt. On the one hand, Darwinian evolutionism was the central theory for connecting humanity to the rest of living nature and life to the history of inanimate nature. On the other hand, it shows just how refractory biological explanation has proved to consistent materialist reductionism.

What made Darwin's explanation of evolution by means of wholly natural processes plausible was that his six-year voyage around the world, which widened his sense of the space and time available to the history of life, along with the geological writings of Sir Charles Lyell, had persuaded him that small changes over vast periods of time could bring about the large changes known to have occurred in the history of life. The pressure (a concept he derived from the population theory of Thomas Malthus) that brought about those changes was competition in the struggle for life, resources, and mates, leading to the survival of more viable offspring whose progeny prevailed. The smallest change could produce an advantage, and advantages accumulated over long periods of time.

Even so, some phenomena tested Darwin's faith in natural selection, and he had to reassure himself and his readers. He presented a brave, even slightly taunting, front. The natural theologian William Paley, whose writings had delighted him at Cambridge and which he said were the only part of the university course which "was of the least use to me in the education of my mind," had suggested that contemplation of the eye was a cure for atheism: such a beautiful and complex structure could only have been contrived by an Omnipotent Designer.[7] Darwin took up this point in his chapter "Difficulties on Theory" in a section entitled "Organs of Extreme Perfection and Complication."

> To suppose that the eye, with all its inimitable contrivances for adjusting the focus to different distances, for admitting different amounts of light, and for the correction of spherical and chromatic aberration, could have been formed by natural selection, seems, I freely confess, absurd in the highest possible degree. Yet reason tells me, that if numerous gradations from a perfect and complex eye to one very imperfect and simple, each grade being useful to its possessor, can be shown to exist; if further, the eye does vary ever so slightly, and the variations be inherited, which is certainly the case; and if any variation or modification in the organ be ever useful to an animal under changing conditions of life, then the difficulty of believing that a perfect and complex eye could be formed by natural selection, though insuperable by our imagination, can hardly be considered real.[8]

In private Darwin was less confident. He wrote to Asa Gray in 1860, "I remember well the time when the thought of the eye made me cold all over, but I have got over this stage of the complaint, and now small trifling particulars of structure often make me very uncomfortable. The sight of a feather in a peacock's tail, whenever I gaze at it, makes me sick!"[9]

We see here a great scientist teetering on the edge of granting the theistic argument, then called the argument from design or natural theology and revived in our own time as Intelligent Design. Indeed, as time went on he granted that other factors played a role in evolutionary change, but all were natural, not supernatural. The same cannot be said of the codiscoverer of evolution by natural selection, Alfred Russel Wallace, who sent him a letter from the Malay Archipelago in 1858, just as Darwin was finally getting down to writing his "big book," never published in his lifetime, called *Natural Selection*. Wallace's short account contained, quite literally, the chapter headings of Darwin's magnum opus. A compromise was reached, and they published a joint paper and shared credit for the discovery of the theory.

Their relationship had its ironies. Unlike Darwin, Wallace believed that natural selection was a wholly adequate explanation for the history of life up to the origin of man. But in 1870 Wallace wrote an article in which he argued that many features of humanity could not be accounted for by natural selection and the survival of the fittest, for example, the brain, the hairless body, the voice, the moral faculties. He concludes,

> The inference I would draw from this class of phenomena is, that a superior intelligence has guided the development of man in a definite direction, and for a special purpose, just as man guides the development of many animal and vegetable forms . . . we must therefore admit the possibility that, if we are not the highest intelligence in the universe, some higher intelligence may have directed the process by which the human race was developed, by means of more subtle agencies than we are acquainted with.[10]

This is precisely the same argument mounted by nineteenth-century natural theology and current advocates of Intelligent Design: some features of living nature cannot be explained by natural selection, so a higher intelligence is required to account for them.

In the case of man, Wallace was willing to grant that natural selection was not an adequate explanation, a view he held and reiterated up to writing his autobiography in 1905, long after Darwin's death, where he claims that there is a difference in kind, not degree between man and other animals.[11] When he saw Wallace's 1870 paper, Darwin was most disappointed. In *The Descent of Man* the following year, he argued for continuity between man and the higher apes. Wallace, for his part, was disappointed by Darwin's use of what came to be called the metaphor of natural selection because of its voluntarist overtones, a topic to which I return below. This matter is central to my critique of the materialist reductionist program of the modern scientific worldview. Darwin's writing is replete with teleological, voluntarist, and anthropomorphic terms.

Let us look into Darwin's language in some detail. Here is a paragraph that he added to the third edition of *On the Origin of Species*, published in 1861. I have come to believe that the issues raised by this passage are fundamental to the philosophy of science. Here is the text:

Several writers have misapprehended or objected to the term Natural Selection. Some have even imagined that natural selection induces variability, whereas it implies only the preservation of such variations as arise and are beneficial to the being under its conditions of life. No one objects to agriculturists speaking of the potent effects of man's selection; and in this case the individual differences given by nature, which man for some object selects, must of necessity first occur. Others have objected that the term selection implies conscious choice in the animals which become modified; and it has even been urged that, as plants have no volition, natural selection is not applicable to them! In the literal sense of the word, no doubt, natural selection is a false term; but who ever objected to chemists speaking of the elective affinities of the various elements?—and yet an acid cannot strictly be said to elect the base with which it in preference combines. It has been said that I speak of natural selection as an active power or Deity; but who objects to an author speaking of the attraction of gravity as ruling the movements of the planets?

Every one knows what is meant and is implied by such metaphorical expressions; and they are almost necessary for brevity. So again it is difficult to avoid personifying the word Nature; but I mean by Nature, only the aggregate action and product of many natural laws, and by laws the sequence of events as ascertained by us. With a little familiarity such superficial objections will be forgotten.[12]

Let's work our way through this paragraph. First, Darwin says he is not talking about the causes of variability; he's not talking about why species change, why they are modified. He is only talking about the ones that get preserved. Second, he is not a Lamarckian (after what was often mistakenly thought to be the theory of the French biologist, Jean-Baptiste Lamarck). He is not talking about animals or plants striving with the results of effort being inherited—for example, the giraffe stretches its neck to get food, and the acquired changes get inherited. Third, and of interest to us, he plunges into the philosophy of science, and we will be staying with him there for the rest of this essay.

What about "natural selection," what I have called "Darwin's Metaphor"? He says it is not a literal term. Then he says, rightly in my view, that chemists use such terms—"elective affinity" is the example he gives—and that physicists speak of the "attraction of gravity" ruling the movements of the planets. "Every one knows what is meant and is implied by such metaphorical expressions," he says, and "they are almost necessary for brevity." The metaphorical basis of his style is central to my argument, so we will return to this topic below. The next—and closely related—issue is his habit of writing about nature as if it is a conscious agent, that is, anthropomorphically. "So again it is difficult to avoid personifying the word Nature; but I mean by Nature, only the aggregate action and product of many natural laws, and by laws [I only mean] the sequence of events as ascertained by us. With a little familiarity such superficial objections will be forgotten." I don't think they are superficial, and they certainly were not forgotten. They plagued him for the rest of his life. I think that they are the legacy of unresolved problems from the scientific revolution of the sixteenth and seventeenth centuries, problems that Whitehead called "the Achilles heel of the whole system."[13]

What's going on here? Darwin had earlier written to his great mentor and hero, the geologist Charles Lyell, to say that he felt in good company, since Gottfried Leibniz had objected to the law of gravity and claimed that it was opposed to natural religion, because Newton could not show what gravity is. If it's okay for gravity to rule the planets, why can't natural selection rule the history of life? Well, I'd say this makes me think that there are deep and unresolved philosophical issues about phrases in the natural sciences such as "elective affinity" and "gravity" rather than casting doubt on the phrase "natural selection."

We are not talking here about an occasional bit of florid language but about his consistent representation of the concept—natural selection—which binds life to the conditions of existence, binds humanity to the rest of life, and underpins the historicity of life and mind and society. Indeed, if, with Whitehead, we take the concept of organism to be a more fruitful basic unit for metaphysics than matter, force, or particle, Darwin's theory could be seen as the basic, deepest idea in all of science and all of society.

The issue is, therefore, important, to say the least. It has also been—I'd say until recently—a much controverted matter. That is, although Darwin says repeatedly that the analogy between the selection of breeders and farmers and pigeon fanciers was the basis for his analogy to what nature does—natural selection—some historians of biology have claimed that his was not the true path. I think that L. T. Evans's "Darwin's Use of the Analogy between Artificial and Natural Selection" (1984) makes a convincing case for the role of this analogy in the period leading up to Darwin's crucial reading of Malthus—just as Darwin says in his autobiography:

In October 1838, that is, fifteen months after I had begun my systematic inquiry, I happened to read for amusement Malthus on

Population, and being well prepared to appreciate the struggle for existence which everywhere goes on from long-continued observation of the habits of animals and plants, it at once struck me that under these circumstances favourable variations would tend to be preserved, and unfavourable ones to be destroyed. The result of this would be the formation of a new species. Here, then, I had at last got a theory by which to work; but I was so anxious to avoid prejudice, that I determined not for some time to write even the briefest sketch of it.[14]

The phrase "natural selection" and the ways that he wrote about it are absolutely full of voluntaristic, anthropomorphic, taboo words as far as the official rules of science are concerned. One of the cardinal rules of modern science is to avoid explaining things in terms which draw on human intentions and to eschew evaluative language. The abandonment of explanation in terms that draw on analogies to human intentions and which explain in terms of values and purposes (teleology) is, as I've shown above, supposed to set modern science off against earlier forms of explanation of the phenomena of the natural world. There is no escaping the fact that this kind of thinking lies at the heart of Darwin's ideas. Further, I think we can generalize this point to other kinds of science. Doing so can provide insight into, and perhaps even a wistful sort of sympathy for, recent arguments from design.

Darwin stressed this point again in a letter he wrote to his friend, Joseph Hooker. He said in 1844, "I have read heaps of agricultural and horticultural books and have never ceased collecting facts. At last gleams of light have come, and I am almost convinced (quite contrary to the opinion I started with) that species are not (it is like confessing a murder) immutable." He goes on to say, "I believe all these absurd views arise from no one having, as far as I know, approached the subject on the side of variation under domestication, and having studied all that is known about domestication."[15]

We know that in the case of domestic breeders there is a conscious selecting agent. In an important letter in which he revealed his theory to the distinguished American scientist Asa Gray in 1856, Darwin concluded his summary in a passage linking artificial selection intimately with his grand conclusion, relying explicitly on the analogy between artificial and natural selection, expressed in voluntaristic and anthropomorphic terms: "I must say one word more in justification (for I feel sure that your tendency will be to despise me and my crotchets), that all my notions about HOW species change are derived from long continued study of the works of (and converse with) agriculturalists and horticulturalists." After the merest semicolon, he continues, writing of nature as a selecting agent: "and I believe I see my way pretty clearly on the means used by nature to change her species and adapt them to the wondrous and exquisitely beautiful contingencies to which every living being is exposed."[16]

This analogy between human breeders and nature is of crucial significance, since Wallace denied, in their joint paper of 1858—the very paper in which their theory was announced to the world—that any inferences could be drawn about conditions under nature from the study of artificial selection. He says, "We see then, that no inferences as to the permanence of varieties in a state of nature can be deduced from the observation of those occurring among domestic animals."[17]

Let us now notice more of the ways Darwin wrote about natural selection, a term which Evans tells us Darwin began employing after he read a treatise by a man named William Youatt called "Cattle, Their Breeds, Management and Diseases" in March of 1840. Another key concept that has the same overtones is that of "picking," which he used before then and for which, to a considerable extent, "selection" was substituted.[18]

Evans argues that the study of works of this kind was crucial for preparing Darwin for the insight that occurred on reading Malthus in 1838. After this event, or this extended process, Darwin wrote, for example, "It is a beautiful part of my theory, that domesticated races of organisms are made by precisely the same means as species—but [the] latter far more perfectly and infinitely slower." In another place he writes about greyhounds, race horses, and pigeons and then speculates, "Has nature any process analogous[?] [I]f so she can produce great ends." "But how [he is here rehearsing how he is going to spell out his theory]—Make the difficulty apparent by cross-questioning.—even if placed on Isld—if &c &c—Then give my theory.—excellently true theory."[19]

Darwin wrote a pencil sketch of his ideas in 1842, and in 1844 wrote out a more extended one. He was anxious lest he die before going public and left instructions for the publication of the theory if he did. Even though he was so concerned about his mortality, he did not actually publish the theory for another fifteen years and then only in a summary version.

Ten years after writing the 1844 essay he got down to his big book, *Natural Selection*. The first two chapters were on variation under domestication—two hundred pages, which he finished by October 1856. He then wrote the part on natural selection, which he finished at the end of March of 1857. By the middle of June of 1858, he was well along when he received Wallace's letter out of the blue. Wallace's concepts were the same as his own chapter headings—an extraordinary independent discovery of evolution by means of natural selection. He was absolutely appalled by this coincidence, even though Charles Lyell had warned him that Wallace was hot on his heels, thereby catalyzing Darwin's finally getting down to writing what was intended to be his magnum opus. Darwin wrote to Lyell: "I never saw a more striking coincidence; if Wallace had my MS sketch written out in 1842, he could not have made a better short abstract! Even his terms now stand as heads to my chapters."[20]

What actually turned out to be Darwin's biggest book—and the one he wrote even before turning to *The Descent of Man*—was *The Variation of Animals and Plants Under Domestication*: two volumes, three hundred thousand words, published in 1868. He published no other section of *Natural Selection*. Evans concludes from this:

Darwin's recognition of the power of selection in changing organisms was almost entirely due to what he learned of plant and animal breeding. Simple as this may seem now, it involved a bold and brilliant step, namely comprehending that he could use the facts and insights of breeding to understand species in nature. Sir Walter Raleigh and others had previously made this assumption, but the belief had grown during subsequent centuries that domesticated varieties were quite unlike wild species, being much more variable as a result of better nutrition and care and liable to revert in its absence.[21]

Let us get a greater sense of his language. On the first page of chapter 6 of the big book, the chapter on natural selection, Darwin says, "If we reflect on the infinitely numerous & odd variations in all parts of the structure of those few animals & plants, on which man may be said to have experimentised by domestication . . ."[22] He illustrates these with a wealth of examples and then turns to nature. Note the verbs, adverbs, and adjectives. He says,

See how differently Nature acts! . . . She cares not for mere external appearance; she may be said to scrutinise with a severe eye, every nerve, vessel & muscle; every habit, instinct, shade of constitution,—the whole machinery of the organisation. There will be here no caprice, no favouring: the good will be preserved and the bad rigidly destroyed . . . Nature will not commence with some half-monstrous & useless form . . . Nature is prodigal of time & can act on thousands of thousands of generations: she is prodigal of the forms of life . . . Can we wonder then, that nature's productions bear the stamp of a far higher perfection than man's product by artificial selection.[23]

In the introduction to the *Origin*, he says,

At the commencement of my observations it seemed to me probable that a careful study of domesticated animals and cultivated plants would offer the best chance of making out this obscure problem. Nor have I been disappointed; in this and in all other perplexing cases I have invariably found that our knowledge, imperfect though it be, of variation under domestication, afforded the best and safest clue. I may venture to express my conviction of the high value of such studies, although they have been very commonly neglected by naturalists.[24]

In the sketch of 1842 he writes (much of this language gets carried over to the 1844 sketch and to the *Origin*): "But if every part of a plant or animal was to vary . . . and if a being infinitely more sagacious . . ." So we start out with the being man, the selector, the breeder, the horticulturalist, the pigeon fancier, and now he says that

> if a being infinitely more sagacious than man (not an omniscient creator) during thousands and thousands of years were to select all the variations which tended towards certain ends ([or were to produce causes which tended to the same end]), for instance, if he foresaw a canine animal would be better off, owing to the country producing more hares, if he were longer legged and keener sight–greyhound produced [Darwin is writing cryptic notes] . . . Who, seeing how plants vary in garden, what blind foolish man has done in a few years, will deny an all-seeing being in thousands of years could effect (if the Creator chose to do so), either by his own direct foresight or by intermediate means.[25]

In 1857, he wrote to a friend (and reproduced the letter as part of his case for priority over Wallace) of "a being who did not judge by mere external appearances . . . I think it can be shown that there is such an unerring power at work in Natural Selection (the title of my book), which selects exclusively for the good of each organic being."[26] Here we have the cumulative power of natural selection. Indeed, we have the words in the title of this book. How's this for a scientific treatise in a tradition of scientific explanation which is supposed to have banished teleology from science: *On the Origin of Species by Means of Natural Selection, or the Preservation of Favoured Races in the Struggle for Life*? Those terms—"selection," "preservation," "favoured," "struggle," indeed "life" itself—sit uneasily when considered in the light of the reductionist program in modern philosophy of science.

In fact, Darwin says in the chapter "The Struggle for Existence,"

> We have seen that man by selection can certainly produce great results, and can adapt organic beings to his own uses, through the accumulation of slight but useful variations, given to him by the hand of Nature. But Natural Selection . . . is a power incessantly ready for action, and is as immeasurably superior to man's feeble efforts, as the works of Nature are to those of Art.[27]

In the chapter "Natural Selection" he again writes quite comfortably in this vein: "Can the principle of selection, which we have seen is so potent in the hands of man, apply in nature? I think we shall see that it can act most effectually." And also: "As man can produce and certainly has produced a great result by his methodical and unconscious means of selection, what may not nature effect?" He goes on (this is my favorite passage):

> It may be said that natural selection is daily and hourly scrutinising, throughout the world, every variation, even the slightest; rejecting that which is bad, preserving and adding up all that is good; silently and insensibly working, whenever and wherever opportunity offers, at the improvement of each organic being in relation to its organic and inorganic conditions of life.[28]

Here we have a cascade of anthropomorphic descriptions of nature. Darwin is showering the reader with examples of what the critics of Victorian poetry call the "pathetic fallacy,"[29] attributing human emotions and intentions to nature: "acting," "nature's power of selection," "skills," "powers," "visual power," "a power intently watching," "natural selection will pick out with unerring skill."

He is at it again in the "Recapitulation and Conclusion" (I italicize the salient phrases):

> There is no obvious reason why the principles which have *acted* so efficiently under domestication should not have *acted* under nature . . . If then we have under nature variability and *a powerful agent always ready to act and select*, why should we doubt that varia-

tions in any way useful to beings, under their excessively complex relations of life, would be *preserved*, accumulated, and inherited? Why, if man can by patience select variations most useful to himself, should nature fail in *selecting variations useful*, under changing conditions of life, *to her living products*? What limit can be put to *this power, acting during long ages and rigidly scrutinising* the whole constitution, structure, and habits of each creature,—*favouring the good and rejecting the bad*? I can see no limit to *this power, in slowly and beautifully adapting* each form to the most complex relations of life. The theory of natural selection, even if we looked no further than this, seems to me to be in itself probable.[30]

Wallace couldn't stand it. He wrote to Darwin and said,

> I have been so repeatedly struck by the utter inability of numbers of intelligent persons to see clearly, or at all, the self-acting and necessary effects of Natural Selection, that I am led to conclude that the term itself, and your mode of illustrating it, however clear and beautiful to many of us, are yet not the best adapted to impress it on the general naturalist public.[31]

He gives examples of writers who had badly misunderstood Darwin. One of them

> considers your weak point to be that you do not see that "thought and direction are essential to the action of Natural Selection." The same objection has been made a score of times by your chief opponents, and I have heard it as often stated myself in conversation. Now, I think this arises almost entirely from your choice of the term "Natural Selection" and so constantly comparing it in its effects to Man's Selection, and also your so frequently personifying nature as "selecting," as "preferring," as "seeking only the good of the species," etc., etc. To the few this is as clear as daylight, and beautifully suggestive, but to many it is evidently a stumbling-block.[32]

He adds that "people will not understand that all such phrases are metaphors," and suggests that Darwin should instead use "the survival of the fittest"—which seemed to Wallace no different. It was only after Darwin didn't pay a blind bit of attention that Wallace wrote a section in a paper headed "Mr. Darwin's Metaphors Liable to Misconception."[33]

Darwin replied, "I formerly thought, probably in an exaggerated degree, that it was a great advantage to bring into connection natural and artificial selection; this indeed led me to use a term in common, and I still think it some advantage." He said he had just completed a new edition of the *Origin* that was already at the press and concluded with a bit of a tease about Wallace's preferred phrase:

> The term Natural Selection has now been so largely used abroad and at home that I doubt whether it could be given up, and with all its faults I should be sorry to see the attempt made. Whether it will be rejected must now depend "on the survival of the fittest." As in time the term must grow intelligible the objections to its use will grow weaker and weaker.[34]

Many Christian writers took comfort from Darwin's use of the analogy between artificial and natural selection, and argued that it supported the argument from design. For example, in 1869, the distinguished periodical the *Quarterly Review* contained an eloquent defense of design. In it, evolution and even natural selection are seen as perfectly acceptable. The author insists, however, that these depend on design. An extra principle is needed over and above the natural laws, and the argument is supported by reference to Darwin's voluntarist language about natural selection. Darwin's metaphorical language is acknowledged to be figurative, but it is said to help us to see the ultimate dependence of evolution on design. The author, James B. Mozley, concludes,

> So on the field of Nature natural selection, supposing Mr. Darwin's theory of Progress to be true, cannot relieve us from the need of some prior principle, some intelligence, however myste-

rious, which has worked for an end in Nature, and under whose guidance this progress has proceeded . . . He must either make his theory rational, then, by the admission of design; or by the omission of design he must leave it a substantially epicurean hypothesis, accounting for the formation of the animal world by chance. . . .

And so we come round to Paley again.[35]

When, in 1874, Asa Gray wrote that Darwin had done a "great service to Natural Science in bringing back to it Teleology: so that instead of Morphology versus Teleology, we shall have Morphology wedded to Teleology," Darwin commented, "What you say about Teleology pleases me especially, and I do not think any one else has ever noticed the point."[36] Darwin saw no point in banishing teleology and was content, as I have abundantly exemplified, to eschew the strictures of the reductionist paradigm, which banished final causes, purposes, and analogies to human intention.

CONCLUSION

Darwin's use of analogies to human intention, anthropomorphism, teleology, and other explanatory terms that are taboo in the reductionist paradigm of modern scientific explanation makes it clear that biological explanations, to say nothing of explanations in the human sciences, routinely and centrally use concepts that break the rules of materialist reductionist explanation. In a longer essay I have shown in detail how this occurs in central texts in the history of biology and physiology since William Harvey, the discoverer of the circulation of the blood (1628). Harvey was far from a mechanist, however much he has been misdescribed as one by doctrinaire historians of science. The same can be said of the central figure in eighteenth-century physiology, Albrecht von Haller, originator of the concepts of "sensibility" and "irritability" (1751), which remain central to physiology. Elsewhere, I offer further examples in this vein down to the present.[37]

If we return to the critiques of the paradigm of explanation mounted by Whitehead and Burtt, we can use what I have spelled out about Darwin and Wallace, coauthors of the deepest explanatory theory in the biological and human sciences, to assert that the reductionist paradigm of explanation was and remains routinely disobeyed in the biological sciences. The discovery of particulate genetics and the structure and mechanism of DNA have not superseded Darwin's argument or his way of making it. They have only demonstrated the more detailed micromechanisms on which the larger process of natural selection depends. Whitehead and Burtt and the more recent philosophical writings of Peter F. Strawson can be brought together to proffer the claim that the metaphysics of our actual worldview does not rest on matter, motion, and number, on minds and bodies.[38] The concept of a "person" is more philosophically deep than those of mind and body, that of "organism" is more basic than structure and function. The goal of reducing all explanations to matter, motion, and number impoverishes our worldview. Is it any wonder that sincere people reach for theological explanations to husband and celebrate the wonders of nature, life, and human nature and seek to ground them in transcendent processes which continue to use poetic and celebratory language to characterize truth, goodness, and beauty? Appeals to the writings of poets, moralists, and philosophical writers are, in the view of evolutionary reductionists like the evolutionary theorist Richard Dawkins and the so-called Darwinian psychologists, thought to be less deeply explanatory than appeals to competition and other animal instincts and motivations to explain human nature. I hope we can have both the wisdom of the humanities and the findings of scientific research but see nothing to be gained and much to be lost by claiming that the sciences offer us deeper truths and will, in the long run, supersede humanistic reflections.

In my irenic keenness to show the affinity between scientific writers who stop short of zealous reductionism on the one hand and some of the goals of Christian writers on the other, I fear that I may have bent the twig a bit far in favor of the deeper and more laudable goals of those sympathetic to Intelligent Design. If so, I hope the twig settles in an upright position without dogmatism or censorship on either side. If the deep malaise that engenders sympathy for Intelligent Design could be better understood, and if the zealotry of some of the reductionists could be made more apparent and subjected to as severe a philosophical critique as the ones they mount against the fundamentalists and design proponents (though, hopefully, more civilly), then perhaps we could have more balanced and more profound debates. We might take a leaf out of the Victorian debates between science and religion. Many theologians came to see the grandeur in Darwin's view of the history of nature, which he celebrated at the end of *On the Origin of Species*. I quote from the second edition, which added the words I have italicized:

> Thus, from the war of nature, from famine and death, the most exalted object which we are capable of conceiving, namely, the production of the higher animals, directly follows. There is grandeur in this view of life, with its several powers, having been originally *breathed by the Creator into a few* forms or into one; and that, whilst this planet has gone cycling on according to the fixed law of gravity, from so simple a beginning endless forms most beautiful and most wonderful have been, and are being evolved.[39]

One could say that Darwinism provides the bridge between human nature and the sciences. Let's place Darwin in the great scheme of the history of ideas. There have been a number of blows to human arrogance. The Copernican solar system dethroned the earth from being regarded as the center of the universe. Darwinism showed that humanity is not the specially created pinnacle of all living beings. Marxism showed that economic and ideological forces fundamentally condition what humans do. Freud showed that we do not even have access to the greater part of our motivations, which are unconscious. These explanations mitigate our conception of the human species and our planet as central in the firmament and our humanity as adequately characterized by rational intentionality and conscious control over our actions. It is not surprising that many Christians cry out, "Enough!"

But the range and profundity of Darwin's vision also appeals to our sense of grandeur. If we look at Darwin's theory as one of the great ideas in the history of science, we can characterize it as follows. Evolution ranks with gravity, the central concept in physics, and affinity, the key idea in chemistry, as one of the most basic concepts in the sciences. Beyond that, however, evolution by natural selection is a widely applicable theory in two senses. It is the law that binds all of life together and defines its relations with the physical environment—how the history of living nature relates to the history of nature. And, of course, it binds humanity by causal laws to the rest of life and nature. Evolution by natural selection is the process that accounts for the history of living nature, including human nature. It is arguably the most important idea in the history of the natural or human sciences.

In their different ways, to conclude, Darwin and Wallace make more than passable bedfellows to certain tenets of a theistic view of life. They share with Christians a visionary conception of the world. Speaking of bedfellows, it is worth recalling that when Darwin died in 1882, a grateful Anglican nation interred his body in Westminster Abbey. By the time he was laid to rest there, his biographers tell us, he was honored by "the greatest gathering of intellect that was ever brought together in our country." It could be said that natural selection was "'by no means alien to the Christian religion'—not if it was rightly understood, with selection acting 'under Divine intelligence' and governed by 'the spiritual fitness of each man for life hereafter.'" "The Abbey service was to be a visible sign 'of the reconciliation between Faith and Science' . . . The 'new truths' of biology were 'harmless,' their discoverer a secular saint." The burial "proved that the scientists' moral duty in furthering human evolution was best exercised in harmony with the old religious ideas 'upon which the social fabric depends.'" The most emphatic lesson of Darwinism was "the gospel of infinite progress." In his funeral sermon Dean

Farrar said, "This man, on whom years of bigotry and ignorance poured out their scorn, has been called a materialist. I do not see in all his writings one trace of materialism. I read in every line the healthy, noble, well-balanced wonder of a spirit profoundly reverent, kindled into deepest admiration for the works of God." The *Times* was perfectly candid and right to say of Darwin's body that "the Abbey needed it more than it needed the Abbey."[40]

Among the other people honored by being buried there are Geoffrey Chaucer, Oliver Cromwell, John Dryden, George Frideric Handel (composer of *The Messiah*), Samuel Johnson, Alfred Tennyson (who coined the phrase "nature red in tooth and claw"), Rudyard Kipling (who celebrated the survival of the fittest), and the other greatest scientist of all time, Isaac Newton, who lies just a few feet from Darwin. I do not find these strange bedfellows. I want to live in a culture in which all these creative persons can rest in peace together.

NOTES

FOREWORD

1. See, for example, Chris Mooney, *The Republican War on Science* (New York: Basic Books, 2005), which spells out the trend.

2. The statement is printed in *Science* 57 (June 1, 1923): pp. 630–31.

3. Emily Vasquez and Kate Hammer, "Easier Access to Plan B Pill Evokes Praise, and Concern," *New York Times*, Aug. 26, 2006, p. B1.

4. Mooney, *The Republican War on Science*, pp. 223–24. See also Michael Specter, "Political Science: The Bush Administration's War on the Laboratory," *New Yorker*, March 13, 2006, pp. 58–69.

5. I am indebted to Paul Fayter, at York University, in Ontario, Canada, for providing me some years ago with a bibliography of these writings; it then comprised some sixty titles. The papal quotation comes from Gerald L. Schroeder, *Genesis and the Big Bang: The Discovery of Harmony between Modern Science and the Bible* (New York: Bantam Books, 1990), p. 163. The identical point is made in much of the popular writings. See, for example, Robert Jastrow, *God and the Astronomers* (New York: Norton, 1978), p. 116. In this address, the pope specifically acknowledged that the universe is billions of years old, thus, in passing, overriding all literal interpretations of Genesis.

CHAPTER 1. INTRODUCTION

The title of both this essay and the volume was suggested by my son, Charles Comfort. Cynthia Love provided invaluable research assistance. Richard Comfort, Bob Brugger, Carol Greider, Sharon Kingsland, Ron Numbers, Daniel Todes, the other authors of this volume, and two anonymous reviewers improved the manuscript with their careful reading.

1. Stephen Jay Gould, "Darwinian Fundamentalism," *New York Review of Books* 44, no. 10 (1997); Daniel Clement Dennett, *Darwin's Dangerous Idea: Evolution and the Meanings of Life* (New York: Simon & Schuster, 1995), p. 514; Michael Ruse, "Through a Glass, Darkly (Review of Dawkins,

The Devil's Chaplain)," *American Scientist* 91, no. 6 (2003); Joseph P. Kahn, "The Evolution of George Gilder: The Author and Tech-Sector Guru Has a New Cause to Create Controversy With: Intelligent Design," *Boston Globe*, July 27, 2005, p. C1; Phillip E. Johnson, *Darwin on Trial* (Washington, D.C.; Lanham, Md.: Regnery Gateway; distributed to the trade by National Book Network, 1991), p. 14.

2. Michael J. Behe, *Darwin's Black Box: The Biochemical Challenge to Evolution* (New York: Free Press, 1996), pp. 95, 185; Johnson, *Darwin on Trial*, p. 152; David Limbaugh, "The Intelligent Design Bogeyman," Human Events Online, Aug. 5, 2005, www.humaneventsonline.com/article .php?id=8438 (last viewed Feb. 2006); Richard John Neuhaus, "Stifling Intellectual Inquiry," *First Things: The Journal of Religion, Culture, and Public Life* 152 (Apr. 2005): unpaginated; William A. Dembski, *The Design Revolution: Answering the Toughest Questions about Intelligent Design* (Downers Grove, Ill.: InterVarsity Press, 2004), p. 263.

3. Richard Dawkins, *The Ancestor's Tale: A Pilgrimage to the Dawn of Evolution* (Boston: Houghton Mifflin, 2004), p. 13; Dennett, *Darwin's Dangerous Idea*, pp. 17–18. Project Steve: www.natcenscied.org/resources/articles/ 3541_project_steve_2_16_2003.asp.

4. Play "Panda-monium" at www.uncommondescent.com/darwinalia/ panda-monium.swf.

5. Dawkins, "Put Your Money on Evolution," reproduced in Richard Dawkins, *A Devil's Chaplain: Reflections on Hope, Lies, Science, and Love* (Boston: Houghton Mifflin, 2003), pp. 219–20; Daniel Dennett, "Show Me the Science," *The Edge*, Aug. 29, 2005, www.edge.org/3rd_culture/dennett05/ dennett05_index.html (last viewed Sept. 21, 2006).

6. The various drafts of the book that became *Of Pandas and People* were admitted as evidence in the 2005 "Panda trial" in Dover. Scanned images of the pages cited can be found at www2.ncseweb.org/wp/ ?p=80.

7. Kenneth R. Miller, *Finding Darwin's God: A Scientist's Search for Common Ground between God and Evolution* (New York: Cliff Street Books, 1999), p. 164; P. William Davis, Dean H. Kenyon, and Charles B. Thaxton, *Of Pandas and People: The Central Question of Biological Origins* (Dallas, Tex.: Haughton Pub. Co., 1993); Kahn, "The Evolution of George Gilder."

8. Michael Specter, "Political Science," *New Yorker*, Mar. 13, 2006, p. 68.

9. Center for the Renewal of Science and Culture, "The Wedge Strategy," 1999 (cited Apr. 1, 2006), available from www.antievolution.org/features/wedge.html.

10. Charles Krauthammer, "Phony Theory, False Conflict: 'Intelligent Design' Foolishly Pits Evolution against Faith," *Washington Post*, Nov. 18, 2005, p. A23; George F. Will, "Grand Old Spenders," *Washington Post*, Nov. 17, 2005, p. A31.

11. Evan I. Schwartz, *Digital Darwinism: 7 Breakthrough Business Strategies for Surviving in the Cutthroat Web Economy* (New York: Broadway Books, 1999), p. 3.

12. Paul H. Rubin, *Darwinian Politics: The Evolutionary Origins of Freedom* (New Brunswick, N.J.: Rutgers University Press, 2002), p. 30.

13. Brian Boyd, "Evolution and Literature: A Bio-Cultural Approach," *Philosophy and Literature* 29, no. 1 (2005): p. 13; Joseph Carroll, *Literary Darwinism: Evolution, Human Nature, and Literature* (New York: Routledge, 2004), chap. 6; Bradley A. Thayer, *Darwin and International Relations: On the Evolutionary Origins of War and Ethnic Conflict* (Lexington: University Press of Kentucky, 2004), p. 99.

14. Michael McGuire and Alfonso Troisi, *Darwinian Psychiatry* (New York: Oxford University Press, 1998), pp. 230–31.

15. Leah Ceccarelli, *Shaping Science with Rhetoric* (Chicago: University of Chicago Press, 2001), p. 129.

16. Edward O. Wilson, *Consilience: The Unity of Knowledge* (New York: Knopf; distributed by Random House, 1998), p. 244; Michael Shermer, *How We Believe: The Search for God in an Age of Science* (New York: W. H. Freeman, 2000); Pascal Boyer, *And Man Creates God: Religion Explained* (New York: Basic Books, 2001); David Sloan Wilson, *Darwin's Cathedral: Evolution, Religion, and the Nature of Society* (Chicago: University of Chicago Press, 2002); Scott Atran, *In Gods We Trust: The Evolutionary Landscape of Religion* (New York: Oxford University Press, 2002); Daniel Clement Dennett, *Breaking the Spell: Religion as a Natural Phenomenon* (New York: Viking, 2006); Richard Dawkins, *The God Delusion* (Boston: Houghton Mifflin, 2006); L. B. Koenig, M. McGue, R. F. Krueger, and T. J. Bouchard, Jr., "Genetic and Environmental Influences on Religiousness: Findings for

Retrospective and Current Religiousness Ratings," *Journal of Personality* 73, no. 2 (2005): pp. 471–88.

CHAPTER 2. THE ARGUMENT FROM DESIGN

1. W. Paley, *Natural Theology*, in *Collected Works*, vol. 4 (1802; repr. London: Rivington, 1819), p. 1.

2. Ibid., p. 14.

3. J. H. Newman, *The Letters and Diaries of John Henry Newman*, vol. 25, ed. C. S. Dessain and T. Gornall (Oxford: Clarendon Press, 1973), p. 97.

4. Jonathan Barnes, *The Complete Works of Aristotle*, vol. 1 (Princeton, N.J.: Princeton University Press, 1984), p. 997.

5. Augustine, *The City of God against the Pagans*, ed. and trans. R. W. Dyson (Cambridge: Cambridge University Press, 1998), pp. 452–53.

6. St. T. Aquinas, *Summa Theologica*, vol. 1 (London: Burns, Oates and Washbourne, 1952), pp. 26–27.

7. R. Boyle, "A Disquisition about the Final Causes of Natural Things," in *The Works of Robert Boyle*, vol. 5, ed. T. Birch (1688; repr. Hildesheim: Georg Olms, 1966), pp. 397–98.

8. G. Cuvier, *Le règne animal distribué d'aprés son organisation, pour servir de base à l'histoire naturelle des animaux et d'introduction à l'anatomie comparée* (Paris: Déterville, 1817), pp. 1, 6.

9. C. Darwin, *On the Origin of Species* (London: Murray, 1859), p. 63.

10. Ibid., pp. 80–81.

11. R. Dawkins, *A River Out of Eden* (New York: Basic Books, 1995), p. 133.

12. I. Kant, *Critique of Judgement* (1790; repr. New York: Hafner, 1951), p. 25.

13. Darwin, *Origin of Species*, p. 206.

14. C. Darwin, *On the Various Contrivances by which British and Foreign Orchids are Fertilized by Insects, and On the Good Effects of Intercrossing* (London: Murray, 1862), p. 348. Italics added.

15. C. Darwin, Letter to Asa Gray, May 22, 1860, in *The Correspondence of Charles Darwin*, vol. 8, ed. F. Burkhardt, D. M. Porter, J. Browne, and M. Richmond (Cambridge: Cambridge University Press, 1993), pp. 223–24.

16. M. Ruse, *The Darwinian Revolution: Science Red in Tooth and Claw* (Chicago: University of Chicago Press, 1979).

17. H. W. Beecher, *Evolution and Religion* (New York: Fords, Howard, and

Hulbert, 1885), p. 113; F. Temple, *The Relations between Religion and Science* (London: Macmillan and Co., 1884), pp. 452–53.

18. S. J. Gould, and R. C. Lewontin. "The Spandrels of San Marco and the Panglossian Paradigm: A Critique of the Adaptationist Program," *Proceedings of the Royal Society of London, Series B: Biological Sciences* 205 (1979): p. 148.

19. Darwin, Letter to Asa Gray, May 22, 1860.

20. Dawkins, *A River Out of Eden*, pp. 95–96.

21. W. Pannenberg, *Towards a Theology of Nature* (Louisville, Ky.: Westminster/John Knox Press, 1993), p. 16.

CHAPTER 3. THE AERODYNAMICS OF FLYING CARPETS
The full list of authors is Scott F. Gilbert, Anisha Chandra, Nim Cohen, Ben Ewen-Campen, Krystie LaSalle, Katy Lewis, Mamiko Mizutani, and Cynthia Wu. We would like to thank Colin Purrington, Robert Root-Bernstein, Rudy Raff, Dan Kevles, Peter Dobson, and Nathaniel Comfort for their perceptive comments and suggestions. We also wish to thank the Cooper Foundation of Swarthmore College who brought to campus Dr. Kenneth Miller and three of the Dover area high school teachers who refused to read to their classes the pro–Intelligent Design statement handed them by their school board.

1. A. N. Whitehead, *Science and the Modern World* (New York: Macmillan, 1925), p. 181.

2. J. Wells, "Give Me That Old Time Evolution: A Response to the *New Republic*," 2005, www.iconsofevolution.com/embedJonsArticles.php3?id =2933. Italics in the original.

3. The phrase is that of Judge Jones in his verdict at the Intelligent Design trial in Dover, Pennsylvania (*Kitzmiller v. Dover Area School District*, 400 F. Supp. 2d 707 [M.D. Pa 2005], p. 138, www.pamd.uscourts.gov/kitzmiller/kitzmiller_342.pdf). I *was* angry, however, when I found that two of my papers had been cited in the "Bibliography of Supplementary Resources for Ohio Science Instruction" prepared by the staff of the Discovery Institute for lobbying the Ohio State Board of Education against evolution. That one of these papers was published in the journal

Evolution and Development, however, seems to indicate that it was well within the Darwinian mainstream.

4. C. L. Hughes and T. Kaufman, "Hox Genes and the Evolution of the Arthropod Body Plan," *Evolution and Development* 4 (2002): p. 459.

5. S. F. Gilbert, *Developmental Biology*, 8th ed. (Sunderland, Mass.: Sinauer Associates, 2006), p. 749.

6. When I published an article (ibid.) discussing how evolutionary developmental biology could be used to refute ID, Dr. Behe wrote a letter to the editor against it. While his letter contained personal allegations, he did not even try to refute a single piece of evidence that I mentioned. See the exchange at www.nature.com/nrg/journal/v4/n9/abs/nrg1159_fs .html.

7. *Kitzmiller v. Dover Area School District*, 400 F. Supp. 2d 707 (M.D. Pa 2005), trial transcript for Oct. 18, 2005, day 11, p.m., pp. 82–84, www2 .ncseweb.org/kvd/trans/2005_1018_day11_pm.pdf.

8. "Irreducible Complexity and Michael Behe: Do Biochemical Machines Show Intelligent Design?" Talk.Origins, 2006, www.talkorigins.org/ faqs/behe.html.

9. For evidence that Behe is wrong and has known he's been wrong for at least a decade, see, for instance, www.talkorigins.org/faqs/behe.html (Talk.Origins) or Ken Miller's www.millerandlevine.com/km/evol/ design1/article.html ("Answering the Biochemical Argument from Design") and www.millerandlevine.com/km/evol/design2/article.html ("The Flagellum Unspun: The Collapse of 'Irreducible Complexity'"). One can hear a Behe-Miller series of talks (where Behe speaks first, followed by Miller) at the Counterbalance website www.counterbalance .net/perspevo/presmb-frame.html (for Behe), www.counterbalance .net/perspevo/preskm-frame.html (for Miller). These talks were taped at the 2001 Templeton Foundation, Symposium Interpreting Evolution: Scientific and Religious Perspectives, Haverford, Pa. For some of the statements of the creationists and how they twist science, see www .actionbioscience.org/evolution/nhmag.html ("Intelligent Design? A Special Report Reprinted from *Natural History* Magazine"); www .millerandlevine.com/km/evol/index.html ("Evolution Resources"); B. J. Alters and S. Alters, *Defending Evolution: A Guide to the Creation/Evolu-*

tion *Controversy* (Boston: Jones and Bartlett, 2001); www.talkorigins .org/faqs/wells ("*Icons of Evolution* FAQs"); www.nmsr.org/iconanti.htm ("Icons of Anti-Evolution"); M. Pigliucci, *Denying Evolution: Creation, Scientism, and the Nature of Science* (Sunderland, Mass.: Sinauer Associates, 2002).

10. B. A. Rowning, J. Wells, M. Wu, J. C. Gerhart, R. T. Moon, and C. A. Larabell, "Microtubule-Mediated Transport of Organelles and Localization of β-Catenin to the Future Dorsal Side of *Xenopus* Eggs," *Proceedings of the National Academy of Sciences USA* 94 (1997): p. 1224; quote also found at "The Words of the Wells Family," 2005, www.tparents.org/library/ unification/talks/wells/DARWIN.htm. I have simplified the account of how β-catenin becomes localized. For a more detailed review, see Gilbert, *Developmental Biology*, 8th ed., pp. 306–11.

11. A. Sturtevant, "Inheritance of Direction of Coiling in *Limnaea*," *Science* 58 (1923): pp. 269–70.

12. Rowning, Wells, Wu, Gerhart, Moon, and Larabell, "Microtubule-Mediated Transport of Organelles," p. 1224.

13. Ironically, Wells, Behe, and others have claimed loudly and often that the diagrams of Ernst Haeckel (which show the similarities of all vertebrates during the early stages of their development) are fraudulent. Moreover, they claim that these diagrams get repeated so often in evolutionary biology textbooks because evolutionary biologists have no real evidence and must therefore be reduced to using these fraudulent pictures (see J. Wells, *Icons of Evolution: Science or Myth? Why Much of What We Teach about Evolution Is Wrong* [Washington, D.C.: Regnery, 2000] and K. R. Miller and J. Levine, "Haeckel and His Embryos," 2005, www .millerandlevine.com/km/evol/embryos/Haeckel.html). Of course, Haeckel's diagrams were teaching tools, and evolutionary biology was never based on them. (And to say that evolution is false because someone's illustrations are wrong is like saying that Christianity is falsified by Titian's painting a much-revered Madonna who is wearing a red gown that could never have been worn in first-century Judea.) So the ID proponents are doing precisely what they are (falsely) accusing the evolutionary biologists of doing—twisting or ignoring data because their

own ideas are insupportable. Intelligent Design does not respect the evidence.

14. D. Gish, *Evolution? The Challenge of the Fossil Record* (San Diego, Calif.: Creation-Life Publishers, 1985), p. 35. For the link between scientific creationism and ID, see B. Forrest and P. Gross, *Creationism's Trojan Horse* (New York: Oxford University Press, 2004). Robert Root-Bernstein, personal communication.

15. *Kitzmiller v. Dover Area School District*, 400 F. Supp. 2d 707 (M.D. Pa 2005), pp. 66–68, www.pamd.uscourts.gov/kitzmiller/kitzmiller_342.pdf.

16. K. R. Miller and J. Levine, "A True Acid Test," 2005, www.millerand levine.com/km/evol/DI/AcidTest.html; M. Lynch, "Simple Evolutionary Pathways to Complex Proteins," *Protein Science* 14 (2005): pp. 2217–25.

17. W. Dembski, *The Design Revolution: Answering the Toughest Questions about Intelligent Design* (Downers Grove, Ill.: InterVarsity Press, 2004), p. 27.

18. F. Jacob, "Evolution and Tinkering," *Science* 196 (1977): pp. 1161–66.

19. P. Dodson, personal communication.

20. M. Behe, *Darwin's Black Box: The Biochemical Challenge to Evolution* (New York: Free Press, 1996), p. 39.

21. W. J. Gehring and K. Ikeo, "Pax 6: Mastering Eye Morphogenesis and Eye Evolution," *Trends in Genetics* 15 (1999): pp. 371–77.

22. G. Schlosser, "Evolutionary Origins of Vertebrate Placodes: Insights from Developmental Studies and from Comparisons with Other Deuterostomes," *Journal of Experimental Zoology* 304B (2005): pp. 347–99.

23. W. Arthur, *Biased Embryos and Evolution* (New York: Cambridge University Press, 2004); Gilbert, *Developmental Biology*, 8th ed.

24. Gilbert, *Developmental Biology*, 8th ed.

25. Pigliucci, *Denying Evolution*, esp. pp. 236–38.

26. J. Wells and P. Nelson, "Homology: A Concept in Crisis," 2005, www .arn.org/docs/odesign/od182/hobi182.htm; for the use of evolutionary developmental biology against Intelligent Design, see Gilbert, "Opening Darwin's Black Box," pp. 735–41. If we separate praxis from doxy, and look at what the Intelligent Design people do, not what they say, perhaps we will find that they are actually among our most creative Darwinian thinkers. They have combined two of the most interesting areas

of contemporary evolutionary thought—optimal foraging strategy and niche construction—and used them to improve their fitness. It was that great evolutionist Thomas Huxley who observed that the evolutionary struggle in human populations was not for existence but for the enjoyments of existence. "What is often called the struggle for existence in society . . . is a contest, not for the means of existence, but for the means of enjoyment." T. H. Huxley, "Evolution and Ethics: Prolegomena," in *Evolution and Ethics and Other Essays* (New York: Appleton, 1896), p. 40. So these ID proponents, instead of being poor philosophers or scientists struggling to get published and competing for grants, can create their own niche and get rewarded for being first-rate Intelligent Design advocates! They receive more rewards for less labor—a parasitic niche constructed in the integument of evolutionary science. So we should recognize that Intelligent Design proponents may be among our foremost Darwinian practitioners. (And I bet they hate it when I say that!)

27. S. J. Gould, *Wonderful Life* (New York: Norton, 1989), esp. pp. 45–52; 277–91; J. Beatty, "The Evolutionary Contingency Thesis," in *Concepts, Theories, and Rationality in the Biological Sciences*, ed. J. G. Lennox and G. Wolters (Pittsburgh: University of Pittsburgh Press, 1995), pp. 45–81. In my writings on science and society, I have often tried to identify the hype used by both sides of an issue. However, here I find that the evidence is so much in favor of the scientists, that I will not be discussing the scientism of such researchers as Richard Dawkins or Daniel Dennett. Their recent opinions are nothing compared to the egregious distortions and active campaigning of the Intelligent Design lobby. The main criticism I have with their work is that it plays so well into the hands of the religious right, who use it as an example of normative evolutionary biology, thereby allowing them to claim that evolution is a value system, comparable and antagonistic to religion (see M. Bunting, "Why the Intelligent Design Lobby Thanks God for Richard Dawkins," *Guardian* [London], Mar. 27, 2006).

28. Interestingly, Wells (in his above-mentioned website) writes that the Reverend Moon himself chose him to enter biology specifically to fight Darwin's theory, which denied "God's purposeful creative activity." He

realized then that "I should devote my life to destroying Darwinism," and thus began his Ph.D. studies in biology.

29. H. Schell, "Outburst! A Chilling True Story about Emerging-Virus Narratives and Pandemic Social Change," *Configurations* 5 (1997): pp. 93–133; P. Wald, *Contagion: Cultures, Carriers and the Epidemiology of Belonging* (Durham, N.C.: Duke University Press, in press).

30. J. Lederberg, quoted in B. J. Culliton, "Emerging Viruses, Emerging Threat," *Science* 247 (1990): p. 279. See also Susan Nee, "The Great Chain of Being," *Nature* 435 (2005): p. 429.

31. R. Preston, *The Hot Zone* (New York: Random House, 1994), pp. 12–13.

32. D. Nelkin, *The Creation Controversy: Science or Scripture in the Schools* (Boston: Beacon Press, 1982).

33. As mentioned earlier, the Catholic Church has come to terms with evolution, noting that scientists cannot say—within the realm of science—that there is no plan for salvation. Some Jewish biologists use the teachings of Maimonides, who felt that God had so made matter that it could create embryos without angelic intervention in each pregnancy, as their guide to relate science and religion (see Gilbert, *Developmental Biology*, 8th ed.). This seems an especially appropriate model for evolutionary developmental biology, since this discipline finds its mechanisms for evolutionary change within the development of embryonic structures.

CHAPTER 4. THE CLASSROOM CONTROVERSY

1. Phillip E. Johnson, "The Origin of Species Revisited," *Constitutional Commentary* 7 (1990), p. 430.

2. Tamara Henry, "Teachers: What Is Creation?" *USA Today*, July 25, 2001 (contains full text of Senator Santorum's proposal and some discussion of its legislative context).

3. Richard Dawkins, *The Blind Watchmaker* (Burnt Mill, U.K.: Longman, 1986), pp. 4, 241, 251.

4. Ibid., pp. 5–6.

5. Edward O. Wilson, "Intelligent Evolution," *Harvard Magazine* (Fall 2005), 33, excerpt from *From So Simple a Beginning: The Four Great Books of Charles Darwin*, ed. Edward O. Wilson (New York: Norton, 2005).

6. National Academy of Sciences, *Teaching about Evolution and the Nature of Science* (Washington, D.C.: National Academy Press, 1998), p. 58.

7. Laurie Goodstein, "New Light for Creationism," *New York Times*, Dec. 21, 1997, sec. 4, pp. 1, 4.

8. Ibid., p. 4; Richard Dawkins, "Obscurantism to the Rescue," *Quarterly Review of Biology*, 72 (1997): p. 397.

9. *Selman v. Cobb County School District*, 390 F. Supp. 2d 1286, 1309. The Cobb County School District sticker is reprinted at p. 1292.

10. *Kitzmiller v. Dover Area School District*, 400 F. Supp. 2d 707, 735 (M.D. Pa 2005). The Dover Area School District disclaimer is reprinted at pp. 708–9.

11. Ibid., p. 765. Behe's alternative definition for a scientific theory appears in *Kitzmiller v. Dover Area School District*, 400 F. Supp. 2d 707 (M.D. Pa 2005), trial transcript for Oct. 18, 2005, day 11, p.m., p. 34, www2 .ncseweb.org/kvd/trans/2005_1018_day11_pm.pdf.

CHAPTER 5. UNTANGLING DEBATES
ABOUT SCIENCE AND RELIGION

1. Michael Ruse and Daniel Dennett, "Remarkable Exchange between Michael Ruse and Daniel Dennett," Feb. 21, 2006, on Uncommon Descent, www.uncommondescent.com/index.php/archives/844.

2. Charles Darwin, *On the Origin of Species* (London: Murray, 1859), p. 489.

3. Kenneth Chang, "Few Biologists but Many Evangelicals Sign Anti-Evolution Petition," *New York Times*, Feb. 21, 2006, p. 2.

4. Scott Gilbert, *Developmental Biology*, 8th ed. (Sunderland, Mass.: Sinauer Associates, 2006), www.devbio.com; National Institutes of Health, www.nih.gov.

5. Stephen Jay Gould, "Nonoverlapping Magisteria," *Natural History* 106 (March 1997): 16–22.

6. Government Accounting Office on the Government Performance and Results Act, www.gao.gov/new.items/gpra/gpra.htm.

7. Peter Baker and Peter Slevin, "Bush Remarks on 'Intelligent Design' Theory Fuel Debate," *Washington Post*, Aug. 3, 2005, www.washingtonpost .com/wp-dyn/content/article/2005/08/02/AR2005080201686.html.

8. *Kitzmiller v. Dover Area School District*, 400 F. Supp. 2d 707 (M.D. Pa 2005), pp. 1–2, www.pamd.uscourts.gov/kitzmiller/kitzmiller_342.pdf.

9. Ibid., p. 3.

10. Ibid., p. 40.

11. Ibid., p. 46n 7.

12. Ibid., p. 64.

13. Ibid., p. 136.

CHAPTER 6. INTELLIGENT DESIGN

1. R. M. Young, *Darwin's Metaphor: Nature's Place in Victorian Culture* (Cambridge: Cambridge University Press, 1985).

2. Quoted in E. A. Burtt, *The Metaphysical Foundations of Modern Physical Science*, 2nd ed. (London: Routledge and Kegan Paul, 1932), p. 204.

3. A. N. Whitehead, *Science and the Modern World* (Cambridge: Cambridge University Press, 1925; repr. London: Free Association Books, 1985), p. 70.

4. Burtt, *The Metaphysical Foundations of Modern Physical Science*, pp. 318–19.

5. Whitehead, *Science and the Modern World*, pp. 68–69.

6. Burtt, *The Metaphysical Foundations of Modern Physical Science*, pp. 236–37.

7. C. R. Darwin, *The Autobiography of Charles Darwin, 1809–1882: With Original Omissions Restored* (London: Collins, 1958), p. 59.

8. C. Darwin, *On the Origin of Species*, 3rd ed. (London: Murray, 1861), pp. 186–87.

9. F. Darwin, ed., *The Life and Letters of Charles Darwin*, 3rd ed., vol. 2 (London: Murray, 1887), p. 296.

10. A. R. Wallace, "The Limits of Natural Selection as Applied to Man," 1870, reprinted in *Natural Selection and Tropical Nature: Essays on Descriptive and Theoretical Biology* (London: Macmillan, 1891), pp. 194–99, 204.

11. A. R. Wallace, *My Life: A Record of Events and Opinions*, vol. 1 (London: Chapman and Hall, 1905), p. 17.

12. C. R. Darwin, *On the Origin of Species by Means of Natural Selection, or The Preservation of Favoured Races in the Struggle for Life*, 6th ed., with additions and corrections (1859; repr. London: Murray, 1895), pp. 58–59.

13. Whitehead, *Science and the Modern World*, p. 71.

14. Darwin, *The Autobiography of Charles Darwin*, p. 120.

15. Darwin, *Life and Letters*, vol. 2, pp. 23, 29–30.

16. Ibid., vol. 2, pp. 79–80.

17. A. R. Wallace, "On the Tendency of Varieties to Depart Indefinitely from the Original Type," 1858, reprinted in *Natural Selection and Tropical Nature*, p. 31.

18. L. T. Evans, "Darwin's Use of the Analogy between Artificial and Natural Selection," *Journal of the History of Biology* 17 (1984): p. 123.

19. C. R. Darwin, *Charles Darwin's Notebooks, 1836–1844: Geology, Transmutation of Species, Metaphysical Enquiries*, ed. P. H. Barrett, P. J. Gautrey, S. Herbert, D. Kohn, and S. Smith (London: British Museum [Natural History]; Cambridge: Cambridge University Press, 1987), p. 416; Evans, "Darwin's Use of the Analogy," p. 125; Darwin, *Charles Darwin's Notebooks*, p. 430; Evans, "Darwin's Use of the Analogy," p. 126.

20. Darwin, *Life and Letters*, vol. 2, p. 116.

21. Evans, "Darwin's Use of the Analogy," p. 133.

22. C. Darwin, *Charles Darwin's Natural Selection* (Cambridge: Cambridge University Press, 1975), p. 214; Evans, "Darwin's Use of the Analogy," p. 137.

23. Darwin, *Charles Darwin's Natural Selection*, pp. 224–25; Evans, "Darwin's Use of the Analogy," p. 137.

24. Darwin, *On the Origin of Species*, 3rd ed., p. 4.

25. C. D. Darwin and A. R. Wallace, *Evolution by Natural Selection* (Cambridge: Cambridge University Press, 1958), pp. 44, 45–46.

26. Ibid., pp. 264–65.

27. Darwin, *On the Origin of Species*, 3rd ed., p. 61.

28. Ibid., pp. 80, 83, 84.

29. Josephine Miles, *Pathetic Fallacy in the Nineteenth Century* (New York: Octagon, 1965).

30. Darwin, *On the Origin of Species*, 3rd ed., pp. 467, 469.

31. F. Darwin and A. C. Seward, eds., *More Letters of Charles Darwin*, vol. 1 (London: Murray, 1903), p. 267.

32. Ibid., pp. 267–68.

33. Ibid., pp. 269, 268; A. R. Wallace, "Creation by Law," 1868, reprinted in *Natural Selection and Tropical Nature*, pp. 144–45.

34. Darwin and Seward, *More Letters of Charles Darwin*, pp. 270–71.

35. J. Mozley, "The Argument of Design," *Quarterly Review* 127 (1869): pp. 172, 176.

36. Darwin, *Life and Letters*, vol. 3, p. 189, cf. vol. 2, p. 387.

37. R. M. Young, "Persons, Organisms and . . . Primary Qualities," in *History, Humanity and Evolution: Essays for John C. Greene*, ed. J. R. Moore (Cambridge: Cambridge University Press, 1989), pp. 375–401.

38. Peter F. Strawson, *Individuals: An Essay in Descriptive Metaphysics* (London: Methuen, 1959).

39. M. Peckham, ed., *The Origin of Species by Charles Darwin: A Variorum Text* (Philadelphia: University of Pennsylvania Press, 1959), p. 759.

40. A. Desmond and J. R. Moore, *Darwin* (London: Michael Joseph, 1991; repr. Harmondsworth: Penguin, 2004), pp. 672, 671, 671, 674, 676; R. M. Young, *Darwin's Metaphor*, p. 15; Desmond and Moore, *Darwin*, p. 676.

FURTHER READING

CHAPTER 1. INTRODUCTION

Bergman, Gerald. "A Short History of the Modern Creation Movement and the Continuing Modern Cultural Wars." *Journal of American Culture* 26, no. 2 (2003): pp. 243–62.

Larson, Edward J. *Summer for the Gods: The Scopes Trial and America's Continuing Debate over Science and Religion.* New York: Basic Books, 1997.

Numbers, Ronald L. *The Creationists.* Expanded edition. Cambridge, MA: Harvard University Press, 2006.

Park, Hee-Joo. "The Politics of Anti-Creationism: The Committees of Correspondence." *Journal of the History of Biology* 33 (2000): pp. 349–70.

Ruse, Michael. *The Evolution-Creation Struggle.* Cambridge, Mass.: Harvard University Press, 2005.

Woodward, Thomas. *Doubts about Darwin: A History of Intelligent Design.* Grand Rapids, Mich.: Baker Books, 2003.

CHAPTER 2. THE ARGUMENT FROM DESIGN

Forrest, B., and P. R. Gross. *Creationism's Trojan Horse: The Wedge of Intelligent Design.* Oxford: Oxford University Press, 2004.

Hodge, C. *What Is Darwinism?* New York: Scribner's, 1874.

Pennock, R. *Tower of Babel: Scientific Evidence and the New Creationism.* Cambridge, Mass.: MIT Press, 1998.

Ruse, M. *The Darwinian Revolution: Science Red in Tooth and Claw.* Chicago: University of Chicago Press, 1979.

———. *Can a Darwinian Be a Christian? The Relationship between Science and Religion.* Cambridge: Cambridge University Press, 2001.

———. *Darwin and Design: Does Evolution Have a Purpose?* Cambridge, Mass.: Harvard University Press, 2003.

Sarkar, S. *Intelligent Design.* Oxford: Blackwell, 2006.

CHAPTER 3. THE AERODYNAMICS OF FLYING CARPETS

Alters, B. J., and S. Alters. *Defending Evolution: A Guide to the Creation/Evolution Controversy*. Boston: Jones and Bartlett, 2001.

Fernald, R. D. "Evolving Eyes." *International Journal of Developmental Biology* 48 (2004): pp. 701–5.

Gilbert, S. F. *Developmental Biology*, 7th ed. Sunderland, Mass.: Sinauer Associates, 2003.

Kirby, W. *On the Power, Wisdom and Goodness of God as Manifested in the Creation of Animals and in Their History, Habits and Instincts.* Philadelphia: Carey, Lea, & Blanchard, 1836.

Macdonald, R., and S. W. Wilson. "Pax Proteins and Eye Development." *Current Opinion in Neurobiology* 6 (1996): pp. 49–56.

Miller, K. R. "Darwin's Pope?" *Harvard Theological Journal* 33, no. 2 (2005). www.hds.harvard.edu/news/bulletin_mag/articles/33-2_miller.html.

Nelkin, D. *The Creation Controversy: Science or Scripture in the Schools.* Boston: Beacon Press, 1982.

Wawersik, S., and R. L. Maas. "Vertebrate Eye Development as Modeled in Drosophila." *Human Molecular Genetics* 9 (2000): pp. 917–25.

Wells, J. *Icons of Evolution: Science or Myth? Why Much of What We Teach about Evolution Is Wrong.* Washington, D.C.: Regnery, 2000.

CHAPTER 4. THE CLASSROOM CONTROVERSY

Collins, Francis S. *The Language of God: A Scientist Presents Evidence for Belief.* New York: Free Press, 2006. In this book, a leading geneticist who is also an evangelical Christian examines the claims of Intelligent Design and young earth creationism.

Larson, Edward J. *Trial and Error: The American Controversy over Creation and Evolution.* New York: Oxford University Press, 2003. This book offers a survey of the legal battles over the teaching of evolution in American public schools. The author focuses more narrowly on the Scopes trial in his book *Summer for the Gods: The Scopes Trial and*

America's Continuing Debate over Science and Religion. New York: Basic, 1997.

McCalla, Arthur. *The Creationist Debate: The Encounter between the Bible and the Historical Mind.* London: Continuum, 2006. Examining both creation science and Intelligent Design in historical context, this book explores the theological roots of the controversy over the teaching of evolution in the United States.

Numbers, Ronald L. *The Creationists: The Evolution of Scientific Creationism.* Cambridge, Mass.: Harvard University Press, 2006. In this definitive book on the subject, Numbers documents in great detail the origins and spread of the modern American belief in the literal interpretation of the Genesis account of creation, showing it as distinct from but related to the antievolutionism that inspired the Scopes trial.

Ruse, Michael. *The Evolution Wars: A Guide to the Debates.* Santa Barbara, Calif.: ABC-CLIO, 2000. This book offers an excellent introduction to the debate over teaching evolution written by a leading philosopher of science who participated as an expert witness for the plaintiffs challenging the 1981 Arkansas Balanced Treatment Act.

Scopes, John Thomas, and William Jennings Bryan. *The World's Most Famous Court Case: Tennessee Evolution Case.* 1926. Repr., Dayton, Tenn.: Bryan College, 1990. Republished by the college spawned by the Scopes trial, this book (originally published in 1926) includes the complete transcript of the trial, which reads like the drama that it was, and Bryan's proposed closing arguments, which he never delivered at trial but represented the clearest elaboration of his views on Darwinism.

Tompkins, Jerry D., ed. *D-Days at Dayton: Reflections on the Scopes Trial.* Baton Rouge: Louisiana State University Press, 1965. A collection of essays and original source materials by participants in the defense of John Scopes, including extensive excerpts from H. L. Mencken's reports from Dayton and an article by Scopes himself, this book provides insight in the defense's view of the trial.

Walker, Samuel. *In Defense of American Liberties: A History of the ACLU.* New

York: Oxford University Press, 1990. By examining the origins and motivations of the American Civil Liberties Union, this book sheds light on why that organization instigated the Scopes trial and what it gained from doing so.

CHAPTER 5. UNTANGLING DEBATES ABOUT SCIENCE AND RELIGION

American Association for the Advancement of Science. *Science for All Americans*. New York: Oxford University Press, 1991.

———. *Benchmarks for Science Literacy*. New York: Oxford University Press, 1994.

———. "Evolution on the Front Line." 2006. www.aaas.org/news/press_room/evolution/.

Berg, Paul. "Brilliant Science, Dark Politics, Uncertain Law." The Hogan and Hartson Jurimetrics Lecture, Arizona State University Law School, Mar. 1, 2006.

Butler Act in Tennessee. 1925. For the act itself see, for example, www.law.umkc.edu/faculty/projects/ftrials/scopes/tennstat.htm.

Center for Disease Control. "Avian Influenza (Bird Flu)." 2006. www.cdc.gov/flu/avian/.

Clergy Letter Project. "Evolution Sunday." 2006. www.uwosh.edu/colleges/cols/rel_evol_sun.htm.

Dawkins, Richard. *The Blind Watchmaker: Why the Evidence of Evolution Reveals a Universe without Design*. New York: Norton, 1988.

Dennett, Daniel. *Darwin's Dangerous Idea: Evolution and the Meanings of Life*. New York: Simon & Schuster, 1995.

———. *Breaking the Spell: Religion as a Natural Phenomenon*. New York: Viking, 2006.

Gilbert, Scott. *Developmental Biology*, 8th ed. Sunderland, Mass.: Sinauer, 2006.

Maienschein, Jane. *Whose View of Life? Embryos, Cloning, and Stem Cells*. Cambridge, Mass.: Harvard University Press, 2003.

National Academy of Sciences. *Teaching about Evolution and the Nature of Science*. Washington, D.C.: National Academies Press, 1998.

National Institutes of Health. "Stem Cell Basics." http://stemcells.nih
.gov/info/basics.

National Research Council. *National Science Education Standards.*
Washington, D.C.: National Academies Press, 1996.

Ruse, Michael. *Can a Darwinian Be a Christian? The Relation between Science
and Religion.* Cambridge: Cambridge University Press, 2000.

———. *The Evolution-Creation Struggle.* Cambridge: Harvard University
Press, 2005.

Ruse, Michael, and Daniel Dennett. "Remarkable Exchange between
Michael Ruse and Daniel Dennett." www.uncommondescent
.com/index.php/archives/844.

U.S. Department of Education. "No Child Left Behind Act." 2002. www
.ed.gov/nclb/landing.jhtml.

World Health Organization. "Avian Influenza." 2006. www.who.int/
csr/disease/avian_influenza/en/.

CHAPTER 6. INTELLIGENT DESIGN

Beer, Gillian. *Darwin's Plots: Evolutionary Narrative in Darwin, George Eliot
and Nineteenth-Century Fiction.* London: Routledge, 1983.

Darwin, Charles. *Charles Darwin's Natural Selection.* Cambridge:
Cambridge University Press, 1975.

Dawkins, Richard. *A Devil's Chaplain: Selected Essays.* London: Phoenix,
2004.

Dennett, Daniel C. *Darwin's Dangerous Idea: Evolution and the Meaning of
Life.* London: Simon & Schuster, 1995; repr. Harmondsworth:
Penguin, 1996.

Desmond, Adrian, and James Moore. *Darwin: The Life of a Tormented
Evolutionist.* London: Michael Joseph, 1991; repr. Harmondsworth:
Penguin, 2004.

Gillespie, Charles C. *The Edge of Objectivity: An Essay in the History of
Scientific Ideas.* Princeton, N.J.: Princeton University Press, 1960.

Slotten, Ross A. *The Life of Alfred Russel Wallace: The Heretic in Darwin's
Court.* New York: Columbia University Press, 2004.

Young, Robert M. "Science and the Humanities in the Understanding
of Human Nature." Inaugural Lecture as Professor of

Psychotherapy and Psychoanalytic Studies at the Centre for Psychotherapeutic Studies of the University of Sheffield, 2000.

Chapter 6 draws on some of Robert M. Young's earlier writings, which are available online at "Robert M. Young Online Writings," www .human-nature.com/rmyoung/papers/. There is an extensive online archive on Darwin, Darwinism, and Darwinian psychology, including numerous books and papers by Darwin and others, at *Human Nature Review*, www.human-nature.com/.

INDEX

creator. *See* God
credibility in debate, 5
cultural Darwinism, 12–17
Cuvier, Georges, 25–26, 30, 74

Darrow, Clarence, x, 68–69
Darwin, Charles: *Descent of Man, The*, 121; funeral sermon for, 135–36; on human nature, 134; on natural selection, 64, 120–32; *Natural Selection*, 120, 126; *On the Origin of Species*, 26, 86, 121–22, 127–28, 134; on struggle for existence, 26–27; theory of evolution and, 67, 118; *Variation of Animals and Plants under Domestication, The*, 126
Darwinian just-so-stories, 14
Darwinian Politics (Rubin), 13
Darwinian Psychiatry (McGuire and Troisi), 14
Darwinism: anti-Darwinism, x–xi, 65; digital, 13; human nature and, 134; literary, 14; neo-Darwinism, 65; social, 12, 14, 68
Darwin on Trial (Johnson), 3, 4
Darwin's Black Box (Behe), 4, 38, 45
Darwin's Cathedral (Wilson), 15
Darwin's Dangerous Idea (Dennett), 3
Dawkins, Richard: *Ancestor's Tale, The*, 5; anticreationist writings of, 3–6; *Blind Watchmaker, The*, 12, 76, 85; on Darwin's loss of faith, 35; *Devil's Chaplain, The*, 3; on evolutionary theory, 7, 93, 133; natural selection and, 28; scientific response to creation science, 76–77, 85
deism, 64, 67
Dembski, William, 4–6, 38, 49–50; *Design Revolution, The*, 4
Dennett, Daniel, 6, 7, 93; *Breaking the Spell: Religion as a Natural Phenomenon*, 15, 85; *Darwin's Dangerous Idea*, 3
Descartes, René, 24, 114; *Discourse on Method*, 115
Descent of Man, The (Darwin), 121
Design, Argument from, 20–32, 37–38, 110, 112, 120
design, argument to. *See* intelligent design
Design Revolution, The (Dembski), 4
Devil's Chaplain, The (Dawkins), 3
Dialogues Concerning Natural Religion (Hume), 24–25
Digital Darwinism (Schwartz), 13
Discourse on Method (Descartes), 115
Discovery Institute (Washington state), xi, xii, 3; Center for the Renewal of Science and Culture, 9; "Dissent from Darwin" petition, 5, 6, 9, 10–11, 41; scientific credibility of, 5; website, 5; "wedge" document, 10–11; "wedge strategy," 9, 10–11, 41; woman's point of view, 51

"quickening," as definition of beginning of life, 96